Difficult Passages in the Gospels

Difficult Passages in the Gospels

Robert H. Stein

BAKER BOOK HOUSE
Grand Rapids, Michigan 49506

ISBN: 0-8010-8249-8

Printed in the United States of America

To my loving parents, William and Ella Stein, who taught me by example what the love of God was like.

Children, obey your parents in the Lord, for this is right. "Honor your father and mother" (this is the first commandment with a promise), "that it may be well with you and that you may live long on the earth."

Ephesians 6:1–3 (RSV)

Contents

Preface

Several years ago this writer was approached by the denominational periodical, the *Standard*, to do a series on problem passages in the Gospels. I would like to thank the Baptist General Conference for permission to use these articles. Special thanks is given to the editor of the *Standard*, Donald E. Anderson, for approaching me to do this series and for his encouragement and editorial work during this period, and to my wife Joan who read, critiqued, and made suggestions on each of the passages discussed. I also want to thank the faculty secretary, Aletta Whittaker, for her expert typing of the manuscript. It was a pleasure working with her in the production of the final draft.

Unless otherwise stated all biblical quotations come from the Revised Standard Version. Parallel passages presented in synoptic form come from the *Synopsis of the Four Gospels* (United Bible Societies, 1982) or *Gospel Parallels*, edited by Burton H. Throckmorton, Jr. (Nelson, 1967).

Introduction

The New Testament contains four works called Gospels. These Gospels deal with the life and teachings of Jesus of Nazareth, who in the opinion of each of the writers is the "Christ, the Son of God." The fact that the New Testament has four such works is a cause for great joy. How much more blessed is the church by this fourfold testimony to her Lord than if she possessed only one such work.

Yet this very richness is also a cause for consternation. For example, some Gospels speak of a virgin birth and resurrection appearances in Galilee, some do not. The wording of Jesus' sayings varies in the four Gospels. Some place certain events in Jesus' life in a different order. It becomes clear that three of them—Matthew, Mark, and Luke—highly resemble each other both in the order of events and in their wording, whereas the other—John— does not.

As early as the second century A.D. an attempt was made by Tatian in his *Diatessaron* (A.D. 150–170) to combine the four Gospels into a single, comprehensive account. In the third century A.D. Ammonius reportedly utilized the term *harmony* for the first time. His work consisted of the text of the Gospel of Matthew with the parallel passages in the other Gospels listed alongside. The work of Ammonius formed the basis of the famous Canons of Eu-

9

sebius. Eusebius, bishop of Caesarea (A.D. 260–340), using
the work of Ammonius, provided a useful table to help the
reader find the parallel materials in the various Gospels.
The various manuscripts of the Greek New Testament and
numerous printed editions of the Greek New Testament
use it extensively.

Eusebius's table contains ten "canons" or tables of lists.
The Gospels are divided into sections: Matthew contains
355; Mark, 233; Luke, 342; and John, 232. The sections are
numbered consecutively. The first canon lists material
common to all four Gospels. Thus, the first entry is
Matthew—8; Mark—2; Luke—7; John—10. This indicates
that the eighth section of Matthew has a parallel in the
second section of Mark, the seventh section of Luke, and
the tenth section of John. All sections deal with the same
event: the baptism of Jesus. The second canon treats
material common to Matthew, Mark, and Luke; the
third, material common to Matthew, Luke, and John; the
fourth, material common to Matthew, Mark, and John;
the fifth, material common to Matthew and Luke; the
sixth, material common to Matthew and Mark; the seventh, material common to Matthew and John; the eighth,
material common to Luke and Mark; the ninth, material
common to Luke and John; and the tenth contains four
subsections and lists material unique to each Gospel.

The terms *harmony* and *synopsis*, which are frequently
used to describe such works, tend to be misunderstood.
Frequently they are used interchangeably. Even more
confusing is the fact that some writers name their works
harmonies when they would more accurately be termed
synopses. The reverse has also been true. Although an
absolute distinction between the two cannot be made, the
term *synopsis* is best used for works in which the parallel
accounts in the Gospels are placed side by side, usually in
columns. The primary purpose is to place similar materials
side by side for comparison. A harmony seeks to arrange
the material in the four Gospels in an historical order.

Thus it interweaves the various material and places it in chronological order.

Some works utilize both techniques and do not fall neatly into either category. In such instances it is best to classify the work according to its primary purpose. If the aim is to present an historical arrangement of the gospel materials, it is a harmony; if it is primarily for purposes of comparison, it is a synopsis. Thus, the work of Tatian could be termed a harmony, while the works of Eusebius and Ammonius (despite his use of the term harmony) are best called synopses. The term *harmonize* frequently is used to describe an attempt to reconcile different and apparently conflicting accounts and teachings.

One of the problems encountered when a harmony of the Gospels is attempted is that the exact order of the events recorded in the four Gospels cannot always be ascertained. Events and sayings which seem to be identical are located in different places in the Gospels. It sometimes appears that the Evangelists were not interested in the exact order of various events or sayings when they wrote their Gospels. In synopses, even more significant problems arise. Parallel events and sayings often appear with significant variations. How does one deal with such problems?

From the beginning of the Christian Church to the present time various men and women have sought to explain these variations in the context of the inspiration and infallibility of the Scriptures. One of the first and most notable defenders was the greatest theologian of the early church, Augustine. Augustine is known primarily for his theological contributions. But, he was not only a great theologian, he was also a fine New Testament exegete. Around A.D. 400 he wrote *De Concensu Evangelistarum (On the Harmony of the Evangelists)*. Augustine compares the four Gospels and seeks to harmonize them. He tries to demonstrate that ". . . the writers in question [Matthew,

Mark, Luke, and John] do not stand in any antagonism to each other."[1] Augustine later states:

> For this reason let us now rather proceed to examine into the real character of those passages in which these critics suppose the evangelists to have given contradictory accounts . . . ; so that, when these problems are solved, it may also be made apparent that the members in that body have preserved a befitting harmony in the unity of the body itself, not only by identity in sentiment, but also by constructing records consonant with that identity.[2]

Augustine was neither the first nor the last churchman who attempted to defend or harmonize the Gospels. John Calvin states:

> There is no disagreement, first, that one can make no intelligent or apt comment on one of the three Evangelists without comparing the other two. For this reason faithful and skilled commentators have expended most of their efforts on reconciling the three accounts.[3]

Similar purposes lie behind most of the early harmonies. Certainly this is true of Andreas Osiander's *Harmoniae Evangelicae*(1537). Due to his a priori understanding of truth, he believes that the same saying or incident in the life of Jesus must be worded identically and must occur in the same sequence in each Gospel. Any variation in the wording or sequence of parallel accounts means that even virtually indistinguishable passages refer to different sayings or incidents in the life of Jesus. As a result, Osiander argues that Jesus raised Jairus's daughter from the dead on a least two occasions, that Jesus was crowned with thorns at least twice, and that Peter warmed himself at a fire four times. Augustine and Calvin believe that a high view of the inspiration and trustworthiness of the Scriptures does not require such a radical view. William Newcome's *An Harmony of the Gospels in Which the Text is Deposed*

After Le Clerc's General Manner, also attempts to harmonize the accounts. He states, "I have here attempted, after many others, to shew the consistency of the evangelists, and to fix the time and place of the transactions recorded by them."[4] Other works have been written which seek to explain the apparent conflicts found in the Gospels.[5]

The terms *harmonize* and *harmonization* have fallen into disrepute. Some of this may be due to the farfetched and unconvincing harmonizations made in the past by certain scholars. This writer still remembers attending a graduate seminar at a famous German university where a student's explanation was rejected on the grounds that *"Das ist nur Harmonizierung!"* ("That is simply a harmonization!") To reject an explanation because it harmonizes difficult gospel passages is certainly as prejudicial as to accept an explanation on the grounds that it harmonizes these passages. The correctness or incorrectness of an explanation is not dependent on whether or not it harmonizes the disputed passages. It depends on whether that explanation correctly interprets the authors' meanings and logically illustrates that these meanings do not conflict with each other.

This book attempts to follow in the tradition of such scholars as Augustine and Calvin and seeks to establish, if at all possible, a harmony in the passages discussed. This purpose is served best by a forthright openness to the textual data. A prejudicial handling of the data for the sake of establishing the harmony of the Gospels (or for establishing a disharmony) is neither commendable nor, in the case of the former, devout. The Word of God is to be treated reverently even by those who would seek to defend it. The Word of God can and always will defend itself! The evangelical task is, first of all, to understand the meaning of the text. When this is accomplished, the demonstration of its harmonious nature is relatively simple. Newcome states the same thing in the Preface to his harmony: ". . . by thus entering into the manner of the evangelical writers [I take this to mean the authors' meanings], I have endeavoured to make them their own harmonists."[6]

This book contains various representative passages which present certain kinds of difficulties and demonstrates a methodology to deal with them. The first chapter treats the difficulties that arise due to variations in parallel accounts in the Gospels. First, the variations found in parallel accounts of Matthew, Mark, and Luke are discussed. Then the difficulties which result between the parallels in the Synoptic Gospels and the Gospel of John are treated. Chapter two deals with certain difficulties found in the teachings of Jesus. How can some of the sayings of Jesus which seem to conflict at times with what he teaches elsewhere, with his own actions, and with the teachings of the rest of Scripture be explained? Chapter three treats difficulties created by certain actions of Jesus, and chapter four covers selected sayings or predictions of Jesus that do not appear to have come to pass.

The reader should be aware that the author makes no claim of being completely original in his solutions. He is heavily indebted to the work of scholars before him, some of whom have already been mentioned. The numerous references to and quotations of Augustine and Calvin in this work demonstrate this point. An original interpretation or explanation may be offered, but this is not done in order to be original, but simply to deal honestly with the data. On occasion the reader may be disappointed that the author has not found a convincing explanation. This should not be construed as a lack of confidence in the Word of God on the part of the author. Rather it should be interpreted as indicating that the Christian in this life can only "know in part" (I Cor. 13:12). The lack of a satisfactory explanation may be due not to absence of confidence in the Scriptures but to a lack of confidence in possessing sufficient data to resolve the issue. In the majority of instances hopefully the reader should find help and assistance in understanding not only the specific passage or passages discussed, but also in developing a methodology which he or she can extend to similar passages.

Notes

1. Augustine, *De Consensu Evangelistarum*, in *The Nicene and Post-Nicene Fathers*, vol. 6 (New York: Scribners, 1903), I. vii. 10.
2. Ibid. I. xxxv. 54.
3. John Calvin, *A Harmony of the Evangelists Matthew, Mark, and Luke*, ed., David W. and Thomas F. Torrance (Grand Rapids: Eerdmans, 1972), Introduction.
4. William Newcome, *An Harmony of the Gospels in Which the Text is Deposed After Le Clerc's General Manner* (Dublin, 1778), Preface.
5. Two important works written in the last century are J. H. A. Ebrard, *The Gospel History: A Compendium of Critical Investigations in Support of the Historical Character of the Four Gospels*, which appeared in German in 1841 and in English in 1863; and John W. Haley, *Examination of the Alleged Discrepancies of the Bible*, which appeared in 1984. Recently Gleason A. Archer wrote, *Encyclopedia of Bible Difficulties*, (Grand Rapids: Zondervan, 1982). The latter two works, although not exclusively devoted to the Gospels, deal with numerous difficulties in them.
6. Newcome, *An Harmony of the Gospels*, Preface.

1

Difficult Parallel Passages in the Gospels

One of the most valuable tools for the study of the Gospels is a synopsis. In a synopsis, parallel materials are placed side-by-side for comparison. When a synopsis is studied, in the original Greek or in a good translation, it becomes apparent that similar gospel accounts and sayings are seldom identical. Although the differences between the accounts are frequently insignificant and unimportant, at times they appear to present an apparent conflict. How should these differences be treated? Should it be concluded that every parallel incident or saying occurred as many times as the number of parallel accounts?

The material in this chapter deals with ten examples of this type of problem. Seven examples involve differences between parallel accounts in the Synoptic Gospels and three of them treat differences between parallel accounts found in the Synoptic Gospels and the Gospel of John. Each instance deals with both the sayings of Jesus and various events in his life.

Difficult Parallel Passages in the Synoptic Gospels

The Voice from Heaven at Jesus' Baptism

Matthew 3:17	Mark 1:11	Luke 3:22
. . . and lo, a voice from heaven, saying, "This is my beloved Son, with whom I am well pleased."	. . . and a voice came from heaven, "Thou art my beloved Son; with thee I am well pleased."	. . . and a voice came from heaven, "Thou art my beloved Son; with thee I am well pleased."

These parallel accounts present an apparent conflict. This variance does not present any insuperable problem but does illustrate a major principle in the treatment of minor conflicts. The basic issue involves the exact words which were spoken from heaven during the baptism of Jesus. Did the voice say, "Thou art my beloved Son; with thee I am well pleased," as recorded in Mark and Luke, or did the voice say, "This is my beloved Son, with whom I am well pleased," as recorded in Matthew? Or, was the voice addressed to Jesus (Mark and Luke) or to the crowds (Matthew)? That problem is minor, but if it is believed that the Gospels give exact, tape-recorded accounts of what the voice from heaven said, then a problem does exist. However, did Matthew, Mark, and Luke seek to write perfect, tape-recorded accounts of exactly what the voice said?

It may be helpful to note that biblical scholars have wrestled with such questions for many centuries. For example, Augustine was probably the greatest mind in the Christian church between the time of the apostle Paul and the Reformers. Around A.D. 400 Augustine wrote *De Concensu Evangelistarum* (On the Harmony of the Evangelists). Augustine compares the four Gospels and discusses the various parallel accounts in order to harmonize any of the apparent conflicts and discrepancies. This work is still profitable reading both from the perspective of observing Augustine's reverential treatment of the Gospels as well as for his many suggestions on how to harmonize various problems found in the accounts. Many solutions remain convincing today.

Augustine states that "the heavenly voice gave utterance only to one of these sentences. . . ."[1] In other words, Augustine does not seek to resolve the issue by claiming that the voice from heaven spoke both "Thou art my beloved Son . . ." *and* "This is my beloved Son. . . ." (Nor does he seek to resolve the issue by stating that the Greek text of Matthew or Mark and Luke is inaccurate, so that originally all three gospel accounts were alike.) It is not hard to agree with Augustine. To postulate that the voice spoke both statements is not a convincing way to resolve this problem. Second, Augustine points out that despite the differences in wording, each account conveys the same meaning.

> If you ask which of these different modes represents what was actually expressed by the voice, you may fix on whichever you will, provided only that you understand that those of the writers who have not reproduced the self-same form of speech have still reproduced the identical sense intended to be conveyed.[2]

Third, Augustine points out that when an evangelist does change the wording of the voice from heaven, he does so in order to help the reader understand the meaning of those words.

> From this it becomes sufficiently apparent, that whichever of the evangelists may have preserved for us the words as they were literally uttered by the heavenly voice, the others have varied the terms only with the object of setting forth the same sense more familiarly. . . .[3]

Augustine's treatment of this passage has much to teach not only about this particular account but also about other instances in the Gospels where variations occur in the parallel accounts. The facts that the Gospels were written in Greek and that the voice from heaven would have been in Hebrew or Aramaic, the native language of Jesus and the crowds, indicates that no gospel writer was interested in producing a tape-recorded account of the incident.

Augustine also points out that there is no real difference in the accounts. All give the same meaning. If the question were asked, "What did the voice from heaven say at Jesus' baptism?" would not the following answer be perfectly acceptable to all? "It said that Jesus was the Son of God and that God was very pleased with him." Surely the purpose of each Evangelist is to have his readers understand that this Jesus, who was baptized by John, is the Son of God and that God was very pleased with all he did and taught.

If the voice from heaven actually addresses Jesus, this means that Mark's and Luke's accounts are closer to the actual words and that they allow their readers to realize that this Jesus is indeed God's Son. This means that Matthew sought to help his readers by making this application for them. There is no diversity in meaning. Augustine's solution of fifteen centuries ago is still valuable and convincing.

"Blessed are the poor. . . ."

Matthew 5:3	Luke 6:20
"Blessed are the poor in spirit, for theirs is the kingdom of heaven."	"Blessed are you poor, for yours is the kingdom of God."

The Gospels of Matthew and Luke contain two sets of beatitudes. The more famous is found in the opening words of Matthew's Sermon on the Mount (Matt. 5:1–12). Less well known is the parallel account in Luke's Sermon on the Plain (Luke 6:17–23). These passages contain a number of differences. Only one difference is discussed, but in so doing principles will be used that will be helpful for dealing with the other differences.

The term *differences* is used to describe the variations in the two accounts. This term is chosen carefully. Critical scholars tend to use terms such as *discrepancies* or *contradictions* to describe these variations. Such terms prejudge the situation, however, and ought to be avoided. This is especially true at the beginning of an investigation.

The first beatitude, Luke 6:20, reads, "Blessed are you poor, for yours is the kingdom of God." Matt. 5:3, however, reads, "Blessed are the poor in spirit, for theirs is the kingdom of heaven." One explanation frequently used is to state that the two accounts represent two separate speeches by Jesus given at two different times and at two different places. In this instance, Augustine tends to favor this interpretation.[4] This type of explanation, however, has been abused. A sixteenth-century scholar, Andreas Osiander, tends to resolve every minor difference in the Gospels in this manner and as a result argues: Jairus's daughter was raised from the dead on two separate occasions; Jesus was twice crowned with thorns; and Peter warmed himself at a fire four separate times.[5] Luther and Calvin reject these explanations. Yet it cannot be denied that at times such explanations are possible. In this instance the different settings given to the beatitudes (a mountain in Matt. 5:1 and a plain in Luke 6:17) make the possibility of two separate sermons an attractive solution for some.[6]

A fundamental issue that will determine how to view these two accounts involves how the relationship of the Synoptic Gospels to one another is viewed. How can the similarities or "look-alike" character of Matthew, Mark, and Luke be explained? To claim that this is due to God's inspiration does not really answer this question. The Gospel of John is also inspired by God and it is not similar to Matthew, Mark, and Luke! Its vocabulary, content, and form are quite different.

Another attempt to answer this question is to say that Matthew, Mark, and Luke are similar because they record, in chronological order, the events of Jesus' life. Yet it becomes clear that this is not a sufficient explanation. Much of the material in the Synoptic Gospels is arranged on a topical rather than a chronological basis. Mark 1:21–45, for instance, consists of four healing miracles; Mark 2:1–3:6 consists of five pronouncement stories; and Mark 4:1–34 consists of five parables. Matthew arranges the teachings of Jesus into five main sections (5–7; 10; 13; 18; 24–25) that all end in a similar manner.[7] It would appear that topical considerations (placing parables together; listing various miracle stories together; and placing similar teaching material together) are utilized in the Gospels. Augustine states:

> And furthermore, who can fail to perceive that the question as to the precise order in which these words were uttered by the Lord is a superfluous one? [The passage being discussed is Matt. 12:38–42 and the parallel in Luke 11:16, 29–32, but this would also apply to a passage such as the one presently under discussion.] For this lesson also we ought to learn, on the unimpeachable authority of the Evangelists,—namely, that no offence against truth need be supposed on the part of a writer, although he may not reproduce the discourse of some speaker in the precise order in which the person from whose lips it proceeded might have given it; the fact being, that the mere item of the order, whether it be this or that, does not affect the subject-matter itself.[8]

A commonly accepted explanation for the similarity of the Synoptic Gospels is that the Evangelists made use of common written materials. This should not cause any difficulty because the author of Chronicles clearly uses 1 and 2 Samuel and 1 and 2 Kings and Luke (Luke 1:1–4) specifically refers to his investigation of both oral and written materials. Without entering into a total explanation of the "Synoptic problem," it should be pointed out that a commonly accepted explanation of Matthew's and

Luke's similarities in their teaching material and beatitudes is that one used the other (usually Luke used Matthew or, more probably, that both used a common source (which scholars have termed "Q"). If either explanation is accepted (this would not be a rejection of or weakening of the belief that the Gospels of Matthew and Luke are inspired of God) then the explanation of the differences in their beatitudes cannot be explained as two different sermons.

What about this difference between the first beatitude in Matthew and in Luke? Does it not appear that the blessing in Matthew is pronounced on those possessing a spiritual attitude ("being poor in spirit") whereas in Luke it appears to be pronounced on a particular economic strata ("poor")? Some even argue that Matthew "corrupts" Jesus' teaching (which originally, according to Luke, blessed the "poor") and makes it more acceptable to a middle-class church with members not "poor," but "poor in spirit!" Such a negative conclusion is unwarranted.

The basic issue that must first be addressed is the definition of the term *poor* in Luke 6:20. Does it mean economically poor without any additional qualification? Does it mean spiritually poor in the sense of being humble? Does it refer to those who are believers and are economically poor? Before it is proposed that an irreconcilable difference exists between the two beatitudes, it is necessary to understand what the term *poor* meant in the first century A.D.

In the Old Testament the term refers to an economic status and it also is used metaphorically to refer to a spiritual attitude. Psalm 40:17 states, "As for me, I am poor and needy; but the Lord takes thought for me." In Psalm 86:1 and 109:22 the psalmist uses the same two terms to describe himself.[9] It is clear in these instances that the term *poor* is not an economic term because these are "Psalms of David," and the readers of such psalms understood that David, the king, was not economically poor, so that the term should be understood metaphorically. This term is also used in this metaphorical sense in Proverbs 3:34, where it is the opposite of being scornful and is translated humble; Proverbs 16:19, where it is the opposite of being proud and is translated poor; and in 2 Samuel 22:28, where it is the opposite of being haughty and is translated humble. The term *poor* could be and is used in the Old Testament to describe a spiritual state of being humble.[10]

The terminology of translation may assist at this point. It is quite likely that Jesus used the term *poor* without qualification. Luke's use of *poor* is then an exact formal equivalent or a word-for-word translation of this term. Matthew, on the other hand, uses a dynamic equivalent or a thought-for-thought translation. He knew that Jesus metaphorically used the term *poor* for "humble" or "poor in spirit."

Therefore the terms *poor* and *poor in spirit* do not conflict but are two different ways of expressing the idea of humility. However, each Evangelist gives his own emphasis to the term. Luke, more than any other Evangelist, is concerned for the poor and aware of the danger of riches. (This is apparent from Luke 1:53; 6:24; 12:16–21; 16:19–31; 18:18–26; and Acts 4:32–37.) Luke is also aware that the blessedness of the kingdom of God is not exclusively reserved for the economic poor. Zacchaeus, too, shall enter the kingdom (Luke 19:9) even though he is not poor. (Note how Zacchaeus is distinguished from the poor in Luke 19:8.) Luke also mentions rich women (Luke 8:3) and men (Joseph of Arimathea, Luke 23:50–56) who followed Christ. Even the apostle Paul is far from poor according to Acts 28:30 (see also Acts 24:26).

For Luke, however, the term *poor* well designates the blessed followers of Jesus, since many church members come from the lower economic classes (Cf. 1 Cor. 1:26–31; James 2:5; Gal. 2:10 and Rom. 15:26). That the beatitude is addressed to the Christian poor, or the humble believers in the lower classes, is evident from Luke 6:20 (see also Matt. 5:1) where Jesus addresses the beatitudes to the disciples and Luke 6:22 (see also Matt. 5:11) where the blessing is addressed to those hated "on account of the Son of man."

Clearly it is the believing poor, those who are "poor in spirit," who are blessed. Luke's beatitudes are especially precious for such people even as they would be for the disadvantaged and oppressed believers of any age. They are blessed for God gives to such humble people, who trust in Him, the kingdom. But woe to the rich who in their haughtiness, arrogance, and unbelief oppress those poor for there is coming a day of judgment (Luke 6:24)! Matthew chooses not to emphasize this particular aspect of the beatitude.

Rather than seeing a conflict or discrepancy between Matthew's and Luke's accounts of the first beatitude the terms *poor* and *poor in spirit* should be seen as equivalent translations of the term Jesus uses. Each Evangelist emphasizes the particular aspect of Jesus' meaning most needed in his situation. Calvin states, "The metaphor in Luke is unadorned, but . . . Matthew expresses Christ's mind with more clarity."[11] Augustine in dealing with a similar issue, the difference between the form of Jesus' saying in Matthew 12:28 ("But if it is by the Spirit of God that I cast out demons, then the kingdom of God has come upon you.") and in Luke 11:20 ("But if it is by the finger of God that I cast out demons, then the kingdom of God has come upon you.") states:

And the circumstance that Luke here designates the Spirit of God as the finger of God, does not betray any departure from a genuine identity in sense; but it rather teaches us an additional lesson, giving us to know in what manner we are to interpret the phrase "finger of God" wherever it occurs in the Scriptures.[12]

Today many scholars would argue that Luke is closer to the actual words of Jesus, and that Matthew designates in his account what Jesus meant by "the finger of God." However, Augustine's insight remains. There is no "departure from a genuine identity in sense" when one Evangelist gives us "an additional lesson" by his inspired interpretation of what Jesus meant.

One problem remains. This involves the different settings given to the beatitudes by Matthew and Luke. It is possible that Matthew remembers a particular incident in which Jesus taught his disciples on a mountain and uses this scene to form his first collection of Jesus' teachings (Matt. 5–7). Luke may have used another particular incident in which Jesus taught his disciples on a plain for his first collection (Luke 6:17–7:1). This is essentially the view of Calvin who states:

> It should be enough for reverent and humble readers that here, before their eyes, they have set a short summary of the teaching of Christ, gathered from many and various discourses, of which this was the first, where He spoke with His disciples on the true blessedness.[13]

The Healing of the Centurion's Servant

Matthew 8:5–13	Luke 7:1–10
As he entered Capernaum, a centurion came forward to him, beseeching him and saying, "Lord my servant is lying paralyzed at home, in terrible distress." And he said to him, "I will come and heal him."	After he had ended all his sayings in the hearing of the people he entered Capernaum.
	Now a centurion had a slave who was dear to him, who was sick and at the point of death. When he heard of Jesus, he sent to him elders of the Jews, asking him to come and heal his slave. And when they came to Jesus, they besought him earnestly, saying, "He is worthy to have you do this for him, for he loves our nation, and he built us our synagogue." And Jesus went with them. When he was not far from the
But the centurion answered him,	house, the centurion sent friends to

"Lord,
I am not worthy to have you come under my roof;

but only say the word, and my servant will be healed. For I am a man under authority, with soldiers under me; and I say to one, 'Go,' and he goes, and to another, 'Come,' and he comes, and to my slave, 'Do this,' and he does it." When Jesus heard him, he marveled, and said to those who followed him, "Truly I say to you, not even in Israel have I found such faith.

"I tell you, many will come from east and west and sit at table with Abraham, Isaac, and Jacob in the kingdom of heaven, while the sons of the kingdom will be thrown into the outer darkness; there men will weep and gnash their teeth."

And to the centurion Jesus said, "Go; be it done for you as you have believed." And the servant was healed at that very moment.

him, saying to him, "Lord, do not trouble yourself, for I am not worthy to have you come under my roof; therefore I did not presume to come to you. But say the word, and let my servant be healed. For I am a man set under authority, with soldiers under me: and I say to one, 'Go,' and he goes; and to another, 'Come,' and he comes; and to my slave, 'Do this,' and he does it." When Jesus heard this he marveled at him, and turned and said to the multitude that followed him, "I tell you, not even in Israel have I found such faith."

And when those who had been sent returned to the house, they found the slave well.

The two previous passages deal with differences in the various sayings found in the Synoptic Gospels. At this point some of the differences found in various narrative accounts that resemble each other will be discussed. The first example is found in the parallel accounts of the healing of the centurion's servant in Matthew 8:5–13 and Luke 7:1–10. A careful reading of the text raises the question, "Who actually spoke to Jesus? Was it the centurion as Matthew 8:5–9 records or was it the elders of the Jews and the friends as Luke 7:3 and 6 claim? These two accounts of the incident appear to teach contradictory things.

An approach used to harmonize such difficulties has already been mentioned: to claim that these accounts are two different, but similar, incidents. There is little doubt that Jesus often repeats his teachings at different times and places and that he varies them to fit the need of the situation. It is quite possible that similar situations reoccur in the ministry of Jesus. Perhaps Matthew 8:5–13 and Luke 7:1–10 refer to two separate, but similar, incidents in which a servant near death is healed by Jesus.

It seems unlikely that this can be the case. For the circumstances are too similar. In both accounts: the location is Capernaum; a servant of a centurion is involved; Jesus is stopped from entering the centurion's house; Jesus is told, in effect, "Simply say the word and my servant will be healed"; the centurion (or his friends) says "I am a man under authority . . ."; and Jesus marvels at his faith and says, "Not even in Israel have I found such faith." These similarities and the nearly exact wording make it highly unlikely that there are two separate accounts. How could two different centurions even live in Capernaum at the same time? (A centurion was a commander of one hundred soldiers.) One is surprising. Finding two with sick servants, who both have faith and say the same things, seems quite improbable.[14]

If Matthew and Luke contain two versions of the same incident, then who actually spoke to Jesus? The problem can be resolved by the use of a present-day example. If a conversation between the President of the United States and the Premier of Russia, were reported, it could be described in at least two ways. First, the president says in English to his interpreter, "A." The interpreter then says in Russian to the premier, "A." The premier says in Russian to his interpreter, "B," and the interpreter says in English to the president, "B." Second, the president says to the premier, "A," The premier responds "B."

Both descriptions are correct! The last account, which every newspaper report follows, chooses to omit for brevity's sake the role of the interpreter. The other account includes it. It is possible that the Gospel writers follow a similar procedure. Matthew excludes any reference to the elders, whereas Luke includes them in his account.

There is a saying that "As the king—so the messenger." This saying explains that in biblical times a king's messenger was considered an extension of the king. His words were the king's words. His treatment, therefore, was in effect the treatment of the king. With this in mind, it is easier to understand Acts 9:4 ("Saul, Saul, why do you persecute me?"); Matthew 25:37 ("Lord, when did we see thee hungry and feed thee, or thirsty and give thee drink?"); and many others. The messengers, or friends, of the centurion are an extension of him. Their words are the words of the centurion. Thus, the problem dissipates when it is realized that Matthew chose for the sake of brevity, to omit any reference to the intermediate messengers.

This view is confirmed by a careful analysis of the Greek in Luke 7:3 and 6. In Luke 7:3, the text should be translated as follows, "Hearing [singular] concerning Jesus he [the centurion] sent elders of the Jews to him *asking* [singular]. . . ." It should be noted that whereas the elders will speak to Jesus, the participle "asking" is singular. In Luke's mind, although the elders are the ones who actually speak to Jesus, it is the centurion who really asks. In understanding Luke and Matthew, it is the centurion who asks Jesus to heal his servant. Luke 7:6 also should be translated, ". . . the centurion sent [singular] friends saying [singular] to him. . . ." Here again the singular of saying indicates that, in Luke's mind, the centurion says these words to Jesus through the lips of these friends.

The apparent disagreement between Matthew's and Luke's versions disappears when it is understood that Matthew eliminates the reference to the messengers from his account. Calvin comments, "Matthew quite reasonably attributes to him [the centurion] what was done at his request and in his name."[15] Matthew may have done this for the sake of brevity. He had other materials that he wanted to include in his Gospel. The length of a papyrus scroll was limited. (A normal scroll was about 31–32 feet long. Both Matthew and Luke would take up an entire scroll.) Luke, on the other hand, included a reference to them.

Which is correct? Both are correct, for both accurately report what happens between the centurion and Jesus. To be disturbed by Matthew's omission would be to require greater historical exactness in this account than in present-day reports. Neither Matthew nor Luke err in their reports of this incident. It is important to understand how they tell their story of this incident and not demand that they do so in a specific format. After all, they both were inspired of God; we are not.

The Raising of Jairus's Daughter

Matthew 9:18–19, 23–25	Mark 5:21–24, 35–43	Luke 8:40–42, 49–56
	And when Jesus had crossed again in the	Now when Jesus returned,
While he was thus speaking to them,	boat to the other side, a great crowd gathered	
	about him; and he was	the crowd welcomed him, for they were all
behold, a ruler came in	beside the sea. Then came one of the rulers	waiting for him. And there came a man
	of the synagogue, Jairus by name; and	named Jairus, who was a ruler of the
and knelt before him,	seeing him, he fell at his feet, and besought	synagogue; and falling at Jesus' feet he
saying,	him, saying,	besought him to come to his house, for he had
"My daughter has just died; but come and lay your hand on her,	"My little daughter is at the point of death. Come and lay your hands on her, so that she may be made well	an only daughter, about twelve years of age, and she was dying.
and she will live." And Jesus rose and followed him, with his disciples.	and live." And he went with him.	As he went, the people pressed round him.
	While he was still speaking, there came from the ruler's house	While he was still speaking, a man from the ruler's house came

And when Jesus came
to the ruler's house,
and saw the flute
players, and the crowd
making a tumult,
         he said,

"Depart; for the girl is

    not dead but sleep-
ing." And they
laughed at him.

But when the crowd
had been put outside,

he went in
            and took
her by the hand,

and the girl arose.

---

some who said, "Your
daughter is dead. Why
trouble the Teacher any
further?" But ignoring
what they said, Jesus
said to the ruler of the
synagogue, "Do not
fear, only believe."

And he allowed no one
to follow him except
Peter and James and
John the brother of
James.
When they came to the
house of the ruler of
the synagogue, he saw
a tumult, and people
weeping and wailing
loudly. And when he
had entered, he said to
them, "Why do you
make a tumult and
weep? The child is not

dead but sleeping."
And they laughed at
him.

But he put them all
outside, and took the
child's father and
mother and those who
were with him, and
went in where the
child was. Taking her
by the hand he said to
her, "Talitha cumi";
which means, "Little
girl, I say to you,
arise."

And immediately the
girl got up and walked
(she was twelve years
of age), and they were
immediately overcome
with amazement. And

---

and said, "Your
daughter is dead; do
not trouble the Teacher
any more." But Jesus
on hearing this
answered him, "Do not
fear; only believe, and
she shall be well." And
when he came to the
house, he permitted no
one to enter with him,
except Peter and John
and James, and the
father and mother of
the child.

    And all were
weeping and bewailing
her; but
            he said,

"Do not
        weep; for she
is not dead but
sleeping." And they
laughed at him,
knowing that she was
dead. But

           taking her
by the hand he called,
saying,

"Child, arise." And her
spirit returned, and she

got up at once; and he
directed that something
should be given her to
eat. And her parents
were amazed;

he strictly charged	but he charged them to
them that no one	tell no one what had
should know this, and	happened.
told them to give her	
something to eat.	

In seeking to understand why the wording in one account is different from the parallel account in another Gospel, it is helpful to understand not only the theological emphases of the Evangelists but their literary style as well. An example of this is the account of the raising of Jairus's daughter. In Mark's account and in Luke's parallel, a ruler of a synagogue comes to Jesus and asks him to heal his daughter. On the way messengers inform the ruler that she has died, but Jesus encourages the ruler and raises his daughter from the dead. In Matthew's account a ruler comes to Jesus and asks him to bring to life his daughter who has died. Jesus proceeds to his home and raises her from the dead. That this is the same incident is evident not only by the similarity of the stories but by the fact that between the two halves of the story is the account of Jesus' healing of the woman who hemorrhaged for twelve years.

The problems that Matthew's account raises can be resolved once the literary style of Matthew is recognized. If Matthew's treatment of other parallel accounts is compared to Mark's, Matthew's style in telling the story of the raising of Jairus's daughter is better understood. The first account is the healing of the woman who was hemorrhaging. In Mark, the account consists of ten verses (153 words in Greek), whereas in Matthew, the account consists of three verses (48 words in Greek). Matthew obviously abbreviates the story by omitting the following details: the woman spent all her money on doctors, Jesus sensed that healing power had left him, Jesus asked who touched him, the disciples replied that everyone was touching him, and the woman's fear that she would be discovered.

Another example of this tendency of Matthew is found in the account of Jesus' healing of the paralytic. Mark's account consists of twelve verses (196 words in Greek), and Matthew's consists of eight verses (126 words in Greek). Again, Matthew abbreviates the account by leaving out that a crowd had gathered in the home and that the friends had to dig up the roof in order to lower the paralytic before Jesus (which was why Jesus saw their faith). Matthew left out material that, while important, is not essential in recounting the miracle.

A final example is found in Luke 7:1–10 and Matthew 8:5–13. The story of the healing of the centurion's servant consists of ten verses (186 words in Greek) in Luke and nine verses (124 words in Greek) in Matthew. (This total excludes verses 11 and 12, which contain a saying of Jesus that Matthew adds at this point but is found elsewhere in Luke.) In order to abbreviate the account Matthew omits the role of the centurion's servants and the Jewish elders.

It is clear that Matthew has a tendency to abbreviate the various accounts he incorporates into his Gospel. Often he omits material that is of considerable interest and value but that is not absolutely essential. In his desire to include additional material Matthew was concerned with the limitation of his scroll. Our present Gospel of Matthew contains about as much material as a single scroll could contain. In order to include the birth accounts, the Sermon on the Mount, and various resurrection appearances Matthew abbreviated or eliminated some of the material he found in Mark or his other sources. His abbreviation of the three passages, which total 237 words in Greek, enabled him to include additional material such as Matthew 5:1–18 (251 words). The issue for Matthew was simple: abbreviate these stories or eliminate something like Matthew 5:1–18.

In light of Matthew's tendency toward abbreviation we can better understand what has happened in Matthew 9:18–19, 23–25. Matthew summarized the story of Jesus' raising of Jairus's daughter. He records that a ruler of the synagogue comes to Jesus for help concerning his daughter and that Jesus goes to his home and raises her from the dead. What he omits are various interesting but unnecessary details such as that when Jairus first arrives his daughter is not yet dead. It is interesting to compare the statements of Augustine and Calvin on this passage. Augustine writes:

> But as it was Matthew's object to tell the whole story in short compass, he has represented the father as directly expressing in his request what, it is certain, had been his own real wish, and what Christ actually did.[16]

Calvin states:

> . . . Matthew aiming at brevity mentions in one breath what the others space out more accurately, as it took place. . . . Matthew . . . set down as occurring at the very beginning, what actually happened with the passing of time.[17]

Matthew's account is an inerrant summary of Jesus' raising of Jairus's daughter. Difficulties are encountered if the details of this summary are pressed in a way that Matthew never intended.

The Healing of the Paralytic

Matthew 9:1–8	Mark 2:1–12	Luke 5:17–26
And getting into a boat he crossed over and came to his own city.	And when he returned to Capernaum after some days, it was reported that he was at home. And many were gathered together, so that there was no longer room for them, not even about the door; and he was preaching the word to them.	On one of those days, as he was teaching, there were Pharisees and teachers of the law sitting by, who had come from every village of Galilee and Judea and from Jerusalem; and the power of the Lord was with him to heal.
And behold, they brought to him a	And they came, bringing to him a	And behold, men were bringing

paralytic, lying on his bed;	paralytic carried by four men.	on a bed a man who was paralyzed, and they sought to bring him in and lay him before Jesus; but finding no way to bring him in, because of the crowd, they went up on the roof and let him down with his bed through the tiles into the midst before Jesus.
	And when they could not get near him because of the crowd, they removed the roof above him; and when they had made an opening, they let down the pallet on which the paralytic lay. And	
and when Jesus saw their faith he said to the paralytic, "Take heart, my son; your sins are forgiven." And behold, some of the scribes	when Jesus saw their faith, he said to the paralytic, "My son, your sins are forgiven." Now some of the scribes were sitting there,	And when he saw their faith he said, "Man, your sins are forgiven you." And the scribes and the Pharisees began to question,
said to themselves,	questioning in their hearts,	saying, "Who is this that speaks blasphemies? Who can forgive sins but God only?" When
"This man is blaspheming."	"Why does this man speak thus? It is blasphemy! Who can forgive sins but God alone?" And	
But Jesus, knowing their thoughts,	immediately Jesus, perceiving in his spirit that they thus questioned within themselves, said to them, "Why do you	Jesus perceived their questionings, he answered them, "Why do you question
said,		
"Why do you think evil in your hearts? For which is easier, to say, 'Your sins are forgiven,' or to say, 'Rise and walk'?	question thus in your hearts? Which is easier, to say to the paralytic, 'Your sins are forgiven,' or to say, 'Rise, take up your pallet and walk'?	in your hearts? Which is easier, to say, 'Your sins are forgiven you.' or to say 'Rise and walk'?
But that you may know that the Son of man has authority on earth to forgive sins"—he then said to the paralytic—"Rise, take up your bed and go home."	But that you may know that the Son of man has authority on earth to forgive sins"—he said to the paralytic—"I say to you, rise, take up your pallet and go home."	But that you may know that the Son of man has authority on earth to forgive sins"—he said to the man who was paralyzed—"I say to you, rise, take up your bed and go home."

And he rose	And he rose, and	And immediately he
		rose before them, and
and went home. When	immediately took up	took up that on which
the crowds saw it, they	the pallet and went out	he lay, and went home,
were afraid, and they	before them all; so that	glorifying God. And
glorified God, who had	they were all amazed	amazement seized them
given such authority to	and glorified God,	all, and they glorified
men.		God and were filled
		with awe,
	saying, "We never saw	saying, "We have seen
	anything like this!"	strange things today."

Each Synoptic Gospel contains an account of Jesus'
healing of a paralytic. It is evident that these are parallel
accounts of the same incident rather than two or three
separate but similar incidents. First, Matthew and Mark
both locate their accounts in Capernaum (see Matt. 9:1
with 4:13). Second, the wording in all three accounts is
similar, especially the words of Jesus.[18]

Finally, all three Gospels follow this incident with
the account of Jesus' calling of Matthew-Levi and
with the question of why Jesus' disciples do not fast. In
Mark and Luke these last two accounts are followed
then by the accounts of Jesus' disciples plucking grain
on the Sabbath and Jesus' healing of the man with the
withered hand. It is clear that these three accounts refer
to the same incident in which Jesus healed a paralytic
in Capernaum. Calvin states, "There is no doubt that
the same incident is being told by the three, though
there is a slight variation on points of detail between
them.[19]

The main issue is the apparent conflict between Mark
2:4,"And when they could not get near him because of the
crowd, they removed the roof above him; and when they
had made an opening, they let down the pallet on which
the paralytic lay"; and Luke 5:19, "but finding no way to
bring him in, because of the crowd, they went up on the
roof and let him down with his bed through the tiles into
the midst before Jesus."

The type of roof described in these two accounts presents a problem. Luke clearly refers to a tile roof by stating that the paralytic is lowered "through the tiles." In Mark, however, the paralytic's friends "removed the roof" (literally—"unroofed the roof") and "made an opening."

The conflict is not as evident in the RSV ("made an opening") as it is in the NIV ("digging through it"), NEB ("had broken through"), and NASB ("had dug an opening"). In the Greek, however, the phrase "made an opening" literally translates "dig or gouge out." The term *exoruxantes* frequently is used in Greek literature to refer to gouging out someone's eye, digging a trench, tunneling, or digging a grave (Judg. 16:21; 1 Sam. 11:2; Jos ANT. 6.71; Plutarch, ARTAX. 14,10; Herodotus 2,150; 7, 23; 8, 116; etc.). The verbal root (the verb minus the preposition *ex* which means "out of") is used in Matthew 21:33; Mark 12:1; and Isaiah 5:2 to describe the digging of a winepress in the ground; in Matthew 25:18 to burying one's talent; and in Psalm 94:13 (LXX) to digging a pit.

Mark's use of this term makes it evident that he envisions a typical first-century Galilean home with a central courtyard and steps leading up to a roof made of mud and clay and supported by wooden beams. Such a roof would have to be dug out much like a trench or grave.

On the other hand, Luke envisions a tile roof in which the tile would be lifted up or removed but certainly not dug out. It appears that the Evangelists envision two different types of roofs.

One possible way to reconcile these differences is to deny that the term *exoruxantes* in Mark must be translated "dig up" or "gouge out." This seems difficult. The term clearly means this throughout the literature. Another solution might be to claim that these are two different incidents. But, it was previously pointed out that this is not possible. Perhaps the best way to explain the data is to assume that the house roof is Galilean in construction, as Mark suggests. Luke, in "translating" (not from one language to another but from one environment to another) this incident for the most excellent Theophilus (Luke 1:4), knows that in Theophilus's environment, roofs are constructed of tile. In "translating" this story from Galilee to that environment of Theophilus, how could Luke inform him that the paralytic is lowered through the roof? Digging out a tile roof might not be comprehensible to him. As a result he translated this account by using terms that were meaningful to Theophilus. (One can become sympathetic toward missionary translators of the Scriptures by realizing what Luke might have had to do if Theophilus were an Eskimo!)

Why did Luke recount this story to Theophilus? To explain to him that Jesus saw the faith of the paralytic and his friends because they lowered the paralytic through the roof of the house? Or to explain that Jesus saw their faith because they lowered the paralytic through a roof whose construction materials, unlike that of their own houses, consisted of mud, clay, and wood? If the latter is correct, a conflict exists, because the construction materials do appear to be different in Mark and Luke. On the other hand, if the first view is correct, then there is no conflict. Both Mark and Luke state that Jesus saw the faith of the paralytic and his friends because they lowered him through the roof. Surely this is a better understanding of the purpose and aim of Luke. Luke does not intend to teach Theophilus about construction techniques in Galilee in the first century A.D. Luke is seeking to help Theophilus know the truth of the things he has been taught about Jesus (Luke 1:4), and this involves issues such as Jesus' power to heal and forgive sins. Luke succeeds by telling the story of Jesus and the paralytic who was lowered through the tile.

The Genealogies of Jesus

Matthew 1:1–16	Luke 3:23–38
The book of the genealogy of	Jesus, when he began his

Jesus Christ, the son of David, the son of Abraham. Abraham was the father of Isaac, and Isaac the father of Jacob, and Jacob the father of Judah and his brothers, and Judah the father of Perez and Zerah by Tamar, and Perez the father of Hezron, and Hezron the father of Ram, and Ram the father of Amminadab, and Amminadab the father of Nahshon, and Nahshon the father of Salmon, and Salmon the father of Boaz by Rahab, and Boaz the father of Obed by Ruth, and Obed the father of Jesse, and Jesse the father of David the king. And David was the father of Solomon by the wife of Uriah, and Solomon the father of Rehoboam, and Rehoboam the father of Abijah, and Abijah the father of Asa, and Asa the father of Jehoshaphat, and Jehoshaphat the father of Joram, and Joram the father of Uzziah, and Uzziah the father of Jotham, and Jotham the father of Ahaz, and Ahaz the father of Hezekiah, and Hezekiah the father of Manasseh, and Manasseh the father of Amos, and Amos the father of Josiah, and Josiah the father of Jechoniah and his brothers, at the time of the deportation to Babylon. And after the deportation to Babylon: Jechoniah was the father of Shealtiel, and Shealtiel the father of Zerubbabel, and Zerubbabel the father of Abiud, and Abiud the father of Eliakim, and Eliakim the father of Azor, and Azor the father of Zadok, and Zadok the father of Achim, and Achim the father of Eliud, and Eliud the father of Eleazar, and Eleazar the father of Matthan, and Matthan the father of Jacob, and Jacob the father of Joseph the husband of Mary, of whom Jesus was born, who is called Christ.

ministry, was about thirty years of age, being the son (as was supposed) of Joseph, the son of Heli, the son of Matthat, the son of Levi, the son of Melchi, the son of Jannai, the son of Joseph, the son of Mattathias, the son of Amos, the son of Nahum, the son of Esli, the son of Naggai, the son of Maath, the son of Mattathias, the son of Semein, the son of Josech, the son of Joda, the son of Joanan, the son of Rhesa, the son of Zerubbabel, the son of Shealtiel, the son of Neri, the son of Melchi, the son of Addi, the son of Cosam, the son of Elmadam, the son of Er, the son of Joshua, the son of Eliezer, the son of Jorim, the son of Matthat, the son of Levi, the son of Simeon, the son of Judah, the son of Joseph, the son of Jonam, the son of Eliakim, the son of Melea, the son of Menna, the son of Mattatha, the son of Nathan, the son of David, the son of Jesse, the son of Obed, the son of Boaz, the son of Sala, the son of Nahshon, the son of Amminadab, the son of Admin, the son of Arni, the son of Hezron, the son of Perez, the son of Judah, the son of Jacob, the son of Isaac, the son of Abraham, the son of Terah, the son of Nahor, the son of Serug, the son of Reu, the son of Peleg, the son of Eber, the son of Shelah, the son of Cainan, the son of Arphaxad, the son of Shem, the son of Noah, the son of Lamech, the son of Methuselah, the son of Enoch, the son of Jared, the son of Mahalaleel, the son of Cainan, the son of Enos, the son of Seth, the son of Adam, the son of God.

One difficulty with the Gospels is the conflicting genealogies given in the opening chapters of Matthew and Luke.
One difference between these two genealogies, which has
theological significance, is that Matthew 1:1–17 traces the
genealogy of Jesus back to Abraham through three sets of
fourteen descendants. (This may be due to the fact that the
numerical value of the Hebrew consonants *dvd* in David is
fourteen.) Matthew's desire to trace Jesus' lineage back to
David and Abraham is understandable. He seeks to demonstrate that Jesus is the fulfillment of all the hopes and
promises of Israel: in Jesus the Old Testament is fulfilled.[20]

On the other hand it is understandable why Luke,
(3:23–38) addressing a Gentile, Theophilus, is concerned
about demonstrating that Jesus is the fulfillment of the
hopes of all nations, and so he traces Jesus' lineage back to
Adam.

The ability to trace ancestry was quite common in Jesus'
day. Paul knew that he was a Benjaminite (Phil. 3:5).
Josephus reproduced his own genealogical table and mentions that Jews living outside of Israel sent the names of
their children to Jerusalem to be registered in the official
archives. He also mentions that a priest must marry one of
his own race and thus recommends investigating the
genealogy of a prospective wife in the archives.[21] The
Babylonian Talmud refers to a rabbi who investigates the
genealogy of his prospective daughter-in-law and traces it
back to David.[22] The fact that Matthew and Luke record
Jesus' genealogy is not a problem.

However, when the two genealogies are compared the
major problem is immediately apparent. The two listings
of the descendants between Abraham and David essentially are the same, although Luke adds two additional
names: Arni and Admin. From Jesus to David, however,
there are only three names in common: Shealtiel, Zerubbabel, and Joseph. The first five names in Matthew's
listing before Joseph are: Jacob, Matthan, Eleazar, Eliud,
and Achim. The first five in Luke after Joseph are: Heli,

Matthat, Levi, Melchi, and Jannai. Even if Matthan and Matthat refer to the same individual, the differences are apparent.

Over the centuries numerous attempts have been made to resolve this apparent conflict. Aristides, according to Julius Africanus (ca. A.D. 220), explains the differences as due to the fact that Matthew records Jesus' royal genealogy through the kings of Judah, whereas Luke records Jesus' priestly genealogy. Calvin, and more recently J. Gresham Machen, argue that Matthew records the genealogy of Joseph through David, or, the legal lineage, and Luke records the genealogy of Joseph through his real descendents, or, the actual physical lineage.[23] Julius Africanus suggests that Jacob (Matt. 1:15–16) and Heli (Luke 3:23) were half-brothers. After Heli's death Jacob arranged a Levitical marriage and fathered Joseph. Matthew records Jesus' lineage through Jacob (the actual father) and Luke records it through Heli (the legal father—Deut. 25:5–6). Augustine (ca. A.D. 400) suggests that Joseph had two fathers—his natural one, as recorded by Matthew, and an adopted one, as recorded by Luke.

The best attempted solution, however, is that Matthew records the genealogy of Joseph and Luke records the genealogy of Mary. Luke was especially interested in Mary. This is evident by the space he devotes to her and especially by Luke 2:19 and 51 where he speaks of Mary keeping these things in her heart.

Grammatically it is possible to interpret Luke 3:23 in several ways. The RSV and most modern translations, state that "Jesus, when he began his ministry, was about thirty years of age, being the son (as was supposed) of Joseph, the son of Heli. . . ." Another possibility, in the NASB, is, "And when He began His ministry, Jesus Himself was about thirty years of age, being supposedly the son of Joseph, the son of Eli . . ." This translation means that Jesus was about thirty when he began his ministry. Although it was supposed that he was the son of Joseph, in reality this was not true. He was the virgin-born son of Mary, whose father was Heli. Jesus was the son of Heli by Heli's daughter Mary. Luke, in contrast to Matthew's Gospel, gives a genealogy of Mary. This is the neatest and probably the "least unlikely" solution.

How this apparent conflict can be resolved is uncertain. The last suggestion is possible, but not necessarily probable. Most translations agree in separating the parenthetical statement "as was supposed" from "of Joseph." This indicates that the favored interpretation is that Luke's Gospel is also a genealogy of Joseph rather than Mary. Our inability to obtain a perfectly satisfactory solution to this difficulty is frustrating, but should not disturb us too greatly. An evangelical view of Scripture does not claim that the Scriptures can be understood perfectly or infallibly. According to 1 Corinthians 13:12, we know now only in part. We walk by faith and not by sight (2 Cor. 5:7)! Although the teachings of Scripture are infallible, the believer's understanding and interpretation of them is quite prone to fallibility.

Because of this view of the Scriptures, Christians over the centuries sought to reconcile their understanding with its teachings. This is not always possible. To profess uncertainty does not necessarily denote a weak faith. It means that a partial and fallible understanding cannot reconcile particular biblical passages. To profess this uncertainty occasionally is not a weakness of faith but an agreement with what the Scriptures teach: "Now I know in part; then I shall understand fully, even as I have been fully understood" (1 Cor. 13:12).

The Lord's Supper

Matthew 26:26–29	Mark 14:22–25	Luke 22:15–20
		And he said to them, "I have earnestly desired to eat this passover

Now as they were eating, Jesus took bread and blessed, and broke it, and gave it to the disciples and said, "Take, eat; this is my body."

And he took a cup, and when he had given thanks he gave it to them, saying, "Drink of it, all of you; for this is my blood of the covenant, which is poured out for many for the forgiveness of sins.

I tell you I shall not drink again of this fruit of the vine until that day when I drink it new with you in my Father's kingdom."

And as they were eating, he took bread, and blessed, and broke it, and gave it to them, and said, "Take; this is my body."

And he took a cup, and when he had given thanks he gave it to them, and they all drank of it. And he said to them, "This is my blood of the covenant, which is poured out for many.

Truly, I say to you, I shall not drink again of the fruit of the vine until that day when I drink it new in the kingdom of God."

with you before I suffer; for I tell you I shall not eat it until it is fulfilled in the kingdom of God." And he took a cup, and when he had given thanks he said, "Take this, and divide it among yourselves; for I tell you that from now on I shall not drink of the fruit of the vine until the kingdom of God comes." And he took bread, and when he had given thanks he broke it and gave it to them, saying, "This is my body which is given for you. Do this in remembrance of me." And likewise the cup after

supper, saying,

"This cup which is poured out for you is the new covenant in my blood."

The parallel accounts of the Lord's Supper contain a number of difficulties. The first is a textual problem surrounding Luke's account. This difficulty is most apparent in a Greek text of the New Testament, such as the Nestle or United Bible Society texts, but is also apparent in some of the newer translations such as the Revised Standard Version, the New English Bible, and the New American Standard Bible. The issue involves whether Luke 22:19b–20 ("which is given for you. Do this in remembrance of me." And likewise the cup after supper, saying, "This cup which is poured out for you is the new covenant in my blood.") were part of Luke's original text or were later added by a scribe. If these verses are not part of the original text, then Luke's account of the Lord's Supper is most unusual. Instead of the normal order—bread and then cup as found in the accounts in Matthew, Mark, and 1 Corinthians—the order would be cup and bread!

The question remains: are verses 19b–20 part of the original text? Arguments can be presented for both views. These arguments are raised in favor of the view that the original autograph (the Gospel which Luke personally penned, not a subsequent copy) omits verses 19b–20:

1. It is a general rule of textual criticism that the shorter reading is preferred to the longer one. The copyists had a greater tendency to add material to the text than to eliminate it.
2. The verses do not appear to be in Luke's style.
3. The verses are similar to Paul's account of the Lord's Supper in 1 Corinthians 11:24b–25 and may have been added to Luke's account by a copyist who sought to make Luke's version of the Lord's Supper look more like Paul's.
4. The omission of verses 19b–20 is a more difficult reading and it is likely that any scribal error or change would tend to remove a difficulty (add verses 19b–20) than to create one (to remove the verses).

These arguments are raised in favor of the view that verses 19b–20 were part of the original autograph:

1. By far the largest number of Greek manuscripts of the New Testament and, more importantly, the better

Greek manuscripts contain verses 19b–20. Only one Greek manuscript omits verses 19b–20.

2. These verses are found in all of the Greek text types. Their omission is only found in part of the "Western" type of text.

3. It is not difficult to understand how a scribe could have omitted these verses. A cup was mentioned in verses 15–18.

4. The atypical style found in verses 19b–20 may be due to Luke faithfully producing an early tradition of the Lord's Supper which he is content to record. Strong textual support in favor of the longer ending argues for its inclusion in the original autograph of the Gospel. It would appear best to conclude that Luke 22:19b–20 is part of the original text. For some unknown reason it was omitted in a small part of the textual tradition. This conclusion eliminates this textual problem surrounding Luke's account of the Lord's Supper.

Another problem is found in Mark 14:12, "And on the first day of Unleavened Bread, when they sacrificed the passover lamb, his disciples said to him, 'Where will you have us go and prepare for you to eat the passover?'" At first glance this looks like a contradiction of the Old Testament description of the Passover. Leviticus 23:5–6 reads, "In the first month, on the fourteenth day of the month in the evening, is the LORD's passover. And on the fifteenth day of the same month is the feast of unleavened bread to the LORD. . . ." It appears that a clear conflict exists in these accounts. Mark dates the slaying of the Passover lamb on the first day of the Feast of Unleavened Bread. The account in Leviticus 23:5–6 states that this event took place one day earlier. Is it possible that Jesus and the disciples followed a different order in the celebration of the Passover than the Old Testament delineated? Some scholars suggest this. (See pp. 54-58.) If so, then Mark's description of the Lord's Supper does not contain any errors. The issue now involves whether Jesus has the authority to rearrange the Passover timing in this manner. There is evidence that Jesus acts as if he has such authority. Matthew 5 and its many "You have heard that it was said . . ." and "but I say to you. . . ," prove that Jesus claims such authority.

However, a simpler explanation exists for this apparent contradiction. A present-day parallel may help. In many family traditions, "Christmas" begins on the evening of December 24, when Christmas presents are opened. On the other hand, in many family traditions "Christmas" always begins on the morning of December 25, when Christmas presents are opened. In practice Christmas begins at different times even though most families agree that the calendar date for Christmas is December 25.

Similarly, the key for understanding Mark 14:12 is not when the Feast of Unleavened Bread actually begins but how the feast was popularly thought of as beginning. Mark's dating portrays nontechnical dating of the Feast of Unleavened Bread. The feast begins when the ritual search of the house for leaven is made and the Passover lamb is slain (December 24). Technically the Feast of Unleavened Bread begins on the next day (December 25)!

The final problem regarding the Lord's Supper is the apparent conflict surrounding its actual date. Was it a Passover meal celebration as Mark 14:12 and Luke 22:15 suggest? Or was a meal eaten before the Passover as John 18:28 suggests? This question is addressed later in this chapter (see pp. 54-58).

The Audience of the Parable of the Lost Sheep

Matthew 18:12–14	Luke 15:1–7
	Now the tax collectors and sinners were all drawing near to hear him. And the Pharisees and the

"What do you think? If a man has a hundred sheep, and one of them has gone astray, does he not leave the ninety-nine on the mountains and go in search of the one that went astray? And if he finds it, truly,

I say to you, he rejoices over it more than over the ninety-nine that never went astray.
So it is not the will of my Father who is in heaven that one of these little ones should perish."

scribes murmured, saying, "This man receives sinners and eats with them." So he told them this parable: "What man of you, having a hundred sheep, if he has lost one of them, does not leave the ninety-nine in the wilderness, and go after the one which is lost, until he finds it? And when he has found it, he lays it on his shoulders, rejoicing. And when he comes home, he calls together his friends and his neighbors, saying to them, 'Rejoice with me, for I have found my sheep which was lost.' Just so, I tell you, there will be more joy in heaven over one sinner who repents than over ninety-nine righteous persons who need no repentance.

The Gospels often contain identical, or very similar, sayings addressed to different audiences. An example would be the parable of the lost sheep. In Luke's setting, the parable is addressed to the Pharisees and scribes who protest Jesus' practice of eating with tax-collectors and sinners. The parable serves as an apology (in the classical sense; a defense or apologetic) for Jesus' actions. The emphasis of this parable (and of all three parables in Luke 15) can be summarized: "Why are you Pharisees and scribes upset that my ministry brings salvation to the outcasts of society? Why do you not rejoice that the lost sheep/coin/son are being found?" (The two main characters in the parable of the prodigal son are the father and the older, not the younger, brother whose attitude is similar to that of the Pharisees and scribes in Jesus' audience.)

The parable in Matthew 18:12–14 appears to be identical to the parable in Luke 15:3–7. Yet, Matthew's account is addressed to the disciples (Matt. 18:1). It can be argued that Jesus told two similar parables on two different occasions to two different audiences. This is frequently done! Yet several factors go against this explanation. One factor involves how the relationship between these two Gospels is understood. If it is argued that Matthew and Luke are independent works with no literary relationship at all, this view can be maintained. But, if there is some literary relationship (such as Luke using Matthew, which was the common view of the early church, or that both use a similar source of sayings, which is the general view today) then such a view becomes much more difficult. Both explanations assume a single source which almost certainly did not have the parable addressed to both audiences at the same time.

Another difficulty with this view is that there are numerous other biblical examples which contain identical, or at least very similar, sayings addressed to a particular audience in one Gospel and then to a different audience in another Gospel. The following are examples:

Mark 9:50a	Luke 14:34
"Salt is good; but if the salt has lost its saltness, how will you season it?"	"Salt is good; but if salt has lost its taste, how shall its saltness be restored?"

Matthew 6:22–23	Luke 11:34–36
"The eye is the lamp of the body. So, if your eye is sound, your whole body will be full of light; but if your eye is not sound, your whole body will be full of darkness. If then the light in you is darkness, how great is the darkness!	"Your eye is the lamp of your body; when your eye is sound, your whole body is full of light; but when it is not sound, your body is full of darkness. Therefore be careful lest the light in you be darkness. If then your whole body is full of light, having no part dark, it will be wholly bright, as when a lamp with its rays gives you light."

Matthew 7:13–14	Luke 13:24
"Enter by the narrow gate; for the gate is wide and the way is easy, that leads to destruction, and those who enter by it are many. For the	"Strive to enter by the narrow door; for many, I tell you, will seek to enter

gate is narrow and the way is hard,   and will not be able."
that leads to life, and those who find
it are few."

In the first example Mark's account is addressed to the disciples in a house (Mark 9:33). The saying in Luke is addressed to the multitudes (Luke 14:25). In the second and third examples Matthew's sayings are addressed primarily to the disciples (Matt. 5:1), but the saying in Luke 11:34–36 is addressed to the crowds (Luke 11:27, 29) and in Luke 13:24 to the people in the villages and towns on the way to Jerusalem (Luke 13:22).

It seems doubtful that in each case Jesus spoke the same saying twice to two different audiences. A better explanation would be to question the purpose of the Evangelists. Were they merely copyists of Jesus' words? The Evangelists record that they were inspired of God not only to record Jesus' words but also to interpret them for the church. The Holy Spirit caused them to remember not only what Jesus had said but also what he taught them (John 14:25–26). This teaching involved not only remembering to whom Jesus spoke his words but also applying those teachings to new audiences. Were some things that Jesus said to Pharisees and scribes applicable to Christians? If not, they could not be recorded, because no Gospel was written to Pharisees and scribes. If they were, could the Evangelists apply those teachings directly to the church and group them with other similar material? Also were some accounts addressed to the disciples also applicable to the church? Were some things said to men also applicable to women? Were some things said to individuals applicable to the church? Is it only for later readers to make an application of such sayings to a new situation? Could the Evangelists guided by the Spirit do so for us? The easiest explanation of this phenomenon of parallel sayings addressed to different audiences is to see that the Evangelists, through the Spirit, applied the sayings of Jesus to a new situation.

Thus the Spirit led Matthew to take the parable of the lost sheep, originally addressed to Pharisees and scribes (Luke 15:1–2), and to group it with other sayings of Jesus spoken elsewhere in order to form a chapter dealing with life in the church (Matt. 18). This parable is valuable for Christians and not just for Pharisees and scribes. Jesus in his apologetic rebukes any despising of outcasts and demonstrates God's great love for the lost. The church also needs to be reminded of this great love and not to despise her outcasts. As a result, the divine word spoken by Jesus to the Pharisees and scribes becomes a new divine word in Matthew. The Spirit gave to the Evangelist an authoritative and infallible interpretation of this great parable.[24]

Difficult Parallel Passages in the Synoptic Gospels and John

John the Baptist and Elijah

Matthew 17:10–13	Mark 9:11–13	John 1:19–22
And the disciples asked him, "Then why do the scribes say that first Elijah must come?" He replied, "Elijah does come, and he is to restore all things;	And they asked him, "Why do the scribes say that first Elijah must come?" And he said to them, "Elijah does come first to restore all things; and how is it written of the Son of man, that he should suffer many things and be treated with contempt? But I tell you that Elijah has come, and they did to him whatever they pleased, as it is written of him."	And this is the testimony of John, when the Jews sent priests and Levites from Jerusalem to ask him, "Who are you?" He confessed, he did not deny, but confessed, "I am not the Christ." And they asked him, "What then? Are you Elijah?" He said, "I am not." "Are you the prophet?" And he answered, "No."
but I tell you that Elijah has already come, and they did not know him, but did to him whatever they pleased.		
So also the Son of man will suffer at their hands." Then the		

disciples understood
that he was speaking to
them of John the
Baptist.

In the time of Jesus a widespread view existed that the prophet Elijah, who ascended into heaven, would one day return to earth. The primary basis for this expectation was the prophecy in Malachi 4:5–6:

> Behold, I will send you Elijah the prophet before the great and terrible day of the LORD comes. And he will turn the hearts of fathers to their children and the hearts of children to their fathers, lest I come and smite the land with a curse.

This expectation was widespread. There are many references to the return of Elijah in the Gospels (Mark 6:14–15; 8:27–28; 9:11; 15:36) as well as the intertestamental (Sirach 48:10; cf. also Enoch 90:31 in the light of 89:52f.) and rabbinic literature (Shekalim 2.5; Sotah 9.15; Baba Metzia 1.8; Eduyoth 8.7). Within the Gospels an apparent conflict as to the relationship of the coming of John the Baptist and the return of the prophet Elijah is encountered. The problem is immediately apparent when the Synoptic Gospels are compared to the Gospel of John. Matthew 11:14 states, "and if you are willing to accept it, he [John the Baptist] is Elijah who is to come." When asked about the return of Elijah Jesus replies,

> Elijah does come first to restore all things; and how is it written of the Son of man, that he should suffer many things and be treated with contempt? But I tell you that Elijah has come, and they did to him whatever they pleased, as it is written of him (Mark 9:12–13).

Matthew also adds to the account the following editorial comment, "Then the disciples understood that he was speaking to them of John the Baptist" (Matt. 17:13). Yet in

John 1:21 when John the Baptist is asked, ". . . Are you
Elijah?", he replies, "I am not." In the Gospels of Matthew
and Mark Jesus declares that John the Baptist is Elijah and
to this Matthew adds his clear support by his editorial
comment. In the Gospel of John, John the Baptist explicitly
states that he is not Elijah.

One attempted resolution of this conflict argues that the
accounts of Matthew and Mark are correct. John the
Baptist is in fact the fulfillment of Malachi's prophecy. He
fulfills the role of the returning Elijah. On the other hand,
this view argues that the Gospel of John is also correct in
that it accurately records John the Baptist's answer to the
question addressed him. John the Baptist did say that he is
not Elijah, *BUT*, according to this view, he is wrong in
this. Such a resolution of the problem claims to be faithful
to the Scriptural accounts. Each Gospel accurately records
what was said. In the case of John's Gospel, John the
Baptist is not correct in what he said. An example of this
kind of reasoning is found in the Old Testament where
Satan is correctly reported as saying that Eve would not
die if she ate of the tree of the knowledge of good and evil
(Gen. 3:4). Satan's words are clearly incorrect!

Such a solution, however, is not very helpful nor
attractive for at least two reasons. How can it be known
when a gospel writer is accurately recording an incorrect
statement unless the writer reveals this to us in some way?
It is clear that the writer of Genesis 3:4 wants us to
understand that Satan's statement is incorrect because in
the latter part of the chapter and in the following chapters
death plays a prominent part. John, on the other hand,
gives no hint that when John the Baptist denies that he is
the Christ, Elijah, and Jeremiah, he is correct on two of the
answers but is incorrect on the third! Second, it is clear
that John the Baptist consciously dresses in a particular
manner. He was "clothed with camel's hair, and had a
leather girdle around his waist" (Mark 1:6). The Evangelists Matthew and Mark clearly see an allusion to the way

Elijah dressed. Elijah, too, wore camel's hair and a leather girdle (2 Kings 1:8). It is most unlikely that John the Baptist dressed this way by chance. If he intentionally dressed in this manner, it is difficult to deny that he thought that he was in some way fulfilling the role of the one who in the Old Testament dressed in this manner. For these two reasons this attempt to resolve the conflict is not very attractive.

One other attempted resolution, with a long history, involves the differentiation of the "role" of Elijah and the "person" of Elijah. It is clear that the son of Zechariah and Elizabeth (Luke 1:5f.) is not the same person as the prophet Elijah who lived some nine centuries earlier during the days of King Ahab. In essence (ontologically) the "soul" of John the Baptist is not the same "soul" of the prophet Elijah. On the other hand it is clear that the Gospels portray the Baptist as fulfilling the function and role of Elijah. He comes before the great and terrible day of the Lord.[25] That Jesus, himself, interpreted the prophecy of Malachi functionally rather than literally is evident from Matthew 11:14 when he states, "and if you are willing to accept it. . . ." Understood in this manner, there is a sense in which John the Baptist is Elijah and a sense in which he is not.[26]

Perhaps the best way to understand these apparently conflicting passages is to see in John 1:21 a denial on the part of John the Baptist that he is actually the Old Testament Elijah returned from heaven. How else could he have answered the question of whether he was actually the Messiah, Elijah, or Jeremiah? He was in essence none of these. The Gospel of John is correct in recording John the Baptist's answer and John the Baptist is correct in giving this answer. (This also fits the theological emphasis of the Gospel of John which seeks to emphasize the ontological difference between Jesus and John the Baptist and also seeks to maximize the role of the Baptist in bearing witness to the Word becoming flesh.) Despite not being in essence the Elijah who ascended into heaven, the Baptist fulfills the role of Elijah in the prophecy of Malachi 4:5–6 and functions as Elijah by his mission of preparation. Therefore Matthew and Mark are also correct in their portrayal of John the Baptist as the coming Elijah.

Was the Lord's Supper a Passover Meal?

Matthew 26:17–18	Mark 14:12–14	Luke 22:7–11	John 18:28
Now on the first day of Unleavened Bread	And on the first day of Unleavened Bread, when they sacrificed the passover lamb,	Then came the day of Unleavened Bread, on which the passover lamb had to be sacrificed. So Jesus sent Peter and John, saying, "Go and prepare the passover for us,	
the disciples came to Jesus, saying, "Where will you have us prepare for you to eat the passover?"	his disciples said to him, "Where will you have us go and prepare for you to eat the passover?" And he sent two of his disciples,	that we may eat it." They said to him, "Where will you have us prepare it?"	
He said, "Go into the city to a certain one,	and said to them, "Go into the city, and a man carrying a jar of water will meet you; follow him, and wherever he	He said to them, "Behold, when you have entered the city, a man carrying a jar of water will meet you; follow him into the	
and say to him,	enters, say to the householder,	house which he enters, and tell the householder,	Then they led Jesus from the house of Caiaphas to the praetorium. It was early. They themselves did not enter the
'The Teacher says, My time is at hand; I will keep	'The Teacher says, Where is my guest room, where I am to	'The Teacher says to you, Where is the guest room, where I am to	praetorium, so that they might not be defiled, but might eat the passover.

the passover at	eat the passover	eat the passover
your house with	with my	with my
my disciples.'"	disciples?"	disciples?"

Earlier, problems involving the various accounts of the Lord's Supper were discussed. (See pp. 42-46.) A final problem with the Lord's Supper is the confusion concerning the actual date. All Gospel accounts agree that Jesus was crucified on a Friday (Matt. 27:62; Mark 15:42; Luke 23:54; John 19:31, 42), but there is confusion as to whether or not the Lord's Supper was a Passover meal. In the Synoptic Gospels the Lord's Supper is clearly portrayed as a Passover meal. Mark 14:14 states that the two disciples sent by Jesus to prepare for the meal which preceded the Lord's Supper are to say, "The Teacher says, Where is my guest room, where I am to eat the Passover with my disciples?"[27] On the other hand, John reports that Jesus' arrest apparently preceded the Passover. John 18:28 states, "Then they led Jesus from the house of Caiaphas to the praetorium. It was early. They themselves did not enter the praetorium, so that they might not be defiled, but might eat the Passover."[28] According to John, the Passover occurs after Jesus' arrest. How could Jesus, according to the Synoptic Gospels, have eaten the Passover with his disciples before his arrest?

Numerous attempts have been made to explain this apparent discrepancy. Many reveal both the seriousness and reverence with which scholars treat the Word of God. These attempts can be divided into three main classifications:

1. The Synoptic Gospels are correct. According to this view the word *Passover* in John 18:28 does not refer to the eating of the Passover lamb but to the celebration of the entire Feast of Unleavened Bread.[29] The first day of the feast is the Passover. In other words, the

term *passover* refers not to the Passover feast that begins the Feast of Unleavened Bread, but it refers to the eating of the other sacrifices during the feast, the *haghigha*. The main problem with this interpretation is that the term used in John 18:28 is *pascha*. This term certainly would have been understood by the readers of John as referring to the Passover itself.

2. John is correct. It is assumed that Jesus knew that he would die and not be able to eat the Passover. He anticipates the Passover and shares the meal with his disciples one day before its normal time. This explanation contains a number of problems; only two will be mentioned. First, in Mark 14:12 Mark dates the Lord's Supper at the normal time of the Passover celebration. Second, it is extremely doubtful that a private celebration of the Passover, which would still involve the sacrificing of the lambs in the temple by the priesthood of Israel, would be possible. The sacrifice of the Passover lambs was determined by the religious calendar of Israel, not by individual preference.

3. Both the Synoptic Gospels and John are correct. There are a number of variations to this explanation:
   a. In this year the Passover fell on the Sabbath and the Pharisees celebrated the Passover a day earlier, whereas the Sadducees celebrated the Passover at the regular time. The Synoptic Gospels follow the reckoning of the Pharisees and the Gospel of John follows the reckoning of the Sadducees.
   b. That year a dispute arose as to when the month of Nisan (the month in which the Passover occurs) actually began. The Pharisees believed that it began one day earlier than the Sadducees. The Synoptic Gospels follow the Pharisaic reckoning and John follows the Sadducaic.
   c. Since so many sacrifices have to be slain for the Passover, the Galileans celebrate the Passover one

day earlier than the Judeans. The Synoptic Gospels follow the Galilean practice and John follows the Judean.

d. It is known that two different calendars existed in Israel. One was a solar calendar, which the Qumran community followed. The other, which the rest of the Jews followed, was a lunar one. It is possible that different groups in Israel may have celebrated the Passover on two different days.

e. The Jews employed two different ways of calculating when a day began and ended. One group believed that a day is reckoned from daybreak to daybreak. Another believed that it is reckoned from sunset to sunset. According to this theory, the Synoptic Gospels (and Jesus) reckon a day from daybreak to daybreak, whereas John (and the priests) reckon it from sunset to sunset.

All these explanations represent serious and devout attempts to harmonize the conflict between the Synoptic Gospels and John. It is clear that they cannot all be correct. Some appear to have a rather low probability of being correct. In this particular instance, it is doubtful that any of the explanations has a particularly high degree of certainty. The fact that there are so many different explanations suggests that no one explanation is extremely convincing.

It would appear that the evangelical can take one of two positions with regard to this apparent conflict in the dating of the Lord's Supper. First, choose one of the explanations listed above and accept it as a correct explanation. Second, confess the presence of a difficulty which, at the present time, does not have a good explanation. The latter position may be quite frustrating, but at times such a position may be required due to a lack of sufficient information. The evangelical's confidence in the Bible, however, should enable him to accept the fact that there are instances where a satisfactory explanation is not available. The truthfulness of the Bible remains even if its teachings cannot be understood or explained perfectly.

The Hour of the Crucifixion

Mark 15:25	John 19:14–15
And it was the third hour, when they crucified him.	Now it was the day of Preparation of the Passover; it was about the sixth hour. He said to the Jews, "Behold your King!" They cried out, "Away with him, away with him, crucify him!" Pilate said to them, "Shall I crucify your King?" The chief priests answered, "We have no king but Caesar."

Another difficulty in dating the last events in the life of Jesus involves the hour of his crucifixion. Mark 15:25 states that Jesus was crucified at the third hour. John 19:14, however, records that at about the sixth hour Jesus had not been crucified.

Augustine made an attempt to explain this conflict when he states that the "third hour" in Mark 15:25 is not the actual time when Jesus is physically crucified, but the hour in which the Jews cry out that he should be crucified.[30] According to Augustine, at the third hour the Jews crucify Jesus when they say, "Crucify him" (Mark 15:13–14). Therefore, it would be about the sixth hour when the Roman soldiers actually nail Jesus to the cross. Augustine's solution is interesting but unconvincing. If this was Mark's intention, he would place this temporal designation immediately after Mark 15:13–14 rather than after Mark 15:24. Also, grammatical considerations require that the subject "they" in Mark 15:25 must be the same "they" as the previous verse, unless the Evangelist indicates otherwise. The "they" in Mark 15:24 clearly refers to the Roman soldiers!

Other attempts to explain this problem are based on different meanings for the word *hour* (*hora*) in Mark and

John. One suggests that the word *hour* in Mark means "watch." Supposedly the third watch began at noon. Closely related to this explanation is the view that Mark refers to the third hour of Hebrew time (time measured from dawn to dark) and John refers to the sixth hour of Roman time (time measured from midnight on). Since the events of John 19:14f. would require several hours, Jesus was probably crucified at 9 A.M., as Mark records.

There are several strong arguments against these explanations. Concerning the first, a separate Greek word exists which means "watch": *phulake*. If Mark intended to say third watch he could have used this word. He knew of this word because he used it in Mark 6:48! Concerning the latter explanation, it seems clear from John 4:6 that, in this instance, John calculates time according to the Hebrew reckoning. According to this verse Jesus, while passing through Samaria, came to the city of Sychar wearied from his journey and sought water around the sixth hour. By Roman reckoning, this would be approximately 6 A.M. which would leave insufficient time for a wearying journey. According to the Hebrew reckoning, this would be around noon. In light of this it seems that the reference to the sixth hour in John 19:14 should be calculated according to the Hebrew reckoning of time.[31]

Another explanation of this problem involves the possibility of a textual corruption. Again, there are several variations of this approach. A small group of manuscripts for both Mark 15:25 and John 19:14 seek to harmonize these passages. A small number of Greek manuscripts in Mark 15:25 read "sixth" instead of "third," and a few in John 19:14 read "third" instead of "sixth"! In these instances scribes sought to harmonize the two accounts by changing one of them. The vast number of Greek manuscripts, and by far the best, witness to "third" in Mark and "sixth" in John. If the earliest original copies of Mark and John were in agreement, it is hard to understand why there would ever have been any reason for a difference to have arisen.

Another suggestion argues that originally Mark and John agree on the hour but that a copyist later made a mistake. At times, numbers were not written out but given letter equivalents: A = 1, B= 2, etc. The letter for three is a capital *gamma* and for "six" is a capital *digamma*. These look like a capital "F" (for the *digamma*) and a capital "F" minus the middle bar (for the *gamma*). Supposedly, one of these letters was misread by a scribe and the resulting "third" and "sixth" hour conflict arose. It must be pointed out, however, that the best Greek manuscripts all have "third" (Mark) and "sixth" (John) and they also have the numbers spelled out rather than in letter equivalents.

Another attempted resolution along these lines argues that Mark 15:25 is a scribal gloss. It was never part of the inspired text but was added by a scribe. There is no textual evidence for this, however, and it is difficult to understand why a scribe would add a temporal designation which clearly conflicted with the Johannine designation. The scribal tendency was to harmonize such differences, not create them!

A better approach to this problem would be to reconsider the general attitude toward time in the first century A.D. It is clear that the twentieth-century precision toward time, prevalent in Western culture, did not and could not exist in the first century A.D. Such exactness was impossible. Furthermore, the day was commonly divided into four periods: 6 to 9 A.M., 9 to 12 P.M., 12 to 3 P.M., and 3 to 6 P.M. In denoting these periods the hours referred to were the third, the sixth, and the ninth hours. Specific references to time in the New Testament are found in the following passages: Matthew 20:3 (3), 5 (6, 9), 9 (11); 27:45 (6, 9), 46 (9); Mark 15:25 (3), 33 (6, 9), 34 (9); Luke 23:44 (6, 9); John 1:39 (10); 4:6 (6), 52 (7); 19:14 (6); Acts 2:15 (3); 3:1 (9); 10:3 (9), 9 (6), 30 (9); 23:23 (3). There are twenty-three specific references to time in the New Testament and only three (Matt. 20:9; John 1:39, 4:52) use a designation other than 3, 6, or 9 to describe the hour. From this it appears that the usual way of expressing time is to refer to the third, sixth, or ninth hour and that time periods between tend to be rounded off to one of these three designations.

It seems clear that something occurring late in the morning could be rounded off and described by one writer as occurring at the third hour, the 9–12 A.M. period, and by another writer as occurring at the sixth hour, near the 12–3 P.M. period. Calvin argues that for Mark the third hour refers to the ending of the 9–12 A.M. period and for John the sixth hour refers to the beginning of this 12–3 P.M. period.[32] John used the expression "about" to indicate the approximate nature of the time and may have sought to round off the time of Jesus' crucifixion as "about" noon because it was at that time that the passover lambs were to be slain.

When understood in this manner the conflict between the Evangelists is greatly minimized. Even if the third hour occurs between 8–10 A.M. and the sixth hour between 11 A.M. and 1 P.M., the latter part of the first period is close to the beginning of the other. If the time references in these passages are understood as approximate designations in a period where exact time was difficult to achieve, the "third" and "sixth" hour difference should not cause any insurmountable problem.

Notes

1. Augustine, *De Consensu Evangelistarum*, in *The Nicene and Post-Nicene Fathers*, vol. 6 (New York: Scribners, 1903), II.xiv.31.

2. Ibid.

3. Ibid.

4. Ibid., II.xix.45.

5. Andreas Osiander, *Harmonia Evangelicae* (Basel, 1537).

6. For a recent advocate of this view see Gleason L. Archer, *Encyclopedia of Bible Difficulties* (Grand Rapids: Zondervan, 1982), p. 366.

7. Cf. Matthew 7:28; 11:1; 13:53; 19:1; 26:1.

8. Augustine, *De Consensu Evangelistarum*, II.xxxix.86; cf. also II.xiv.29; II.xix.44; II.xxviii.64; II.lxxvii.147.

9. Cf. Psalm 25:16.

10. It is interesting to note that the Qumran community referred to itself at times as the "Congregation of the Poor": 4QpPs 37 2:10; cf.1QpHab 12:3, 6, 10; 1QH 5:22; 1QM 11:9.

11. John Calvin, *A Harmony of the Evangelists Matthew, Mark, and Luke*, ed. David W. and Thomas F. Torrance (Grand Rapids: Eerdmans, 1972), on Matthew 5:3.

12. Augustine, *De Consensu Evangelistarum*, II.xxxvii.85.

13. Calvin, *A Harmony of the Evangelists*, on Matthew 5:1; cf. on Matthew 7:13.

14. For a similar conclusion see Calvin, *A Harmony of the Evangelists*, on Matthew 8:5.

15. Ibid.

16. Augustine, *De Consensu Evangelistarum*, II.xxviii.66.

17. Calvin, *A Harmony of the Evangelists*, on Matthew 9:18.

18. Note also the presence of the same parenthetical comment, "he then said to the paralytic" (Matt. 9:6)/"he said to the paralytic" (Mark 2:10)/"he said to the man who was paralyzed"(Luke 5:24).

19. Calvin, *A Harmony of the Evangelists*, on Matthew 9:1.

20. Cf. Matthew 1:22–23; 2:15, 17–18, 23; 4:14–16; 8:17; 12:17–21; 13:14–15, 35; 21:4–5; 26:54, 56; 27:9–10.

21. See Josephus, *Autobiography* (1) and *Against Apion* (I.7).

22. See the *Babylonian Talmud*, Kethuboth 62b.

23. See J. Gresham Machen, *The Virgin Birth of Christ* (New York: Harper, 1930), pp. 199–209.

24. For a similar approach to these two passages see Calvin, *A Harmony of the Evangelists*, on Matthew 18:12. He assumes that they are the same identical parable and that Matthew and Luke apply the parable to different audiences.

25. Cf. Malachi 4:5–6 with Luke 3:7–9, 16–17.

26. Cf. Calvin, *A Harmony of the Evangelists*, on John 1:21.

27. Cf. Mark 14:16 and Luke 22:15.

28. Cf. John 13:1, 29; 19:14.

29. Cf. 2 Chron. 30:22.

30. Augustine, *De Consensu Evangelistarum*, III.xiii.42.

31. Cf. John 11:9.

32. Calvin, *A Harmony of the Evangelists*, on John 19:14.

2

Difficult Teachings of Jesus

This section investigates some of the more difficult sayings of Jesus. The term *difficult* is not used to denote sayings of Jesus in parallel accounts that appear to contradict each other. These have been investigated in the previous chapter. Nor does this designation mean sayings or teachings of Jesus that are hard to keep. The term *difficult* refers to sayings of Jesus that appear to contradict some of his other teachings or the teachings of the rest of Scripture, or passages which by their literary form appear to be incorrect. Eleven passages will be investigated.

"Do not swear at all" (Matt. 5:34–37)

> But I say to you, Do not swear at all, either by heaven, for it is the throne of God, or by the earth, for it is his footstool, or by Jerusalem, for it is the city of the great King. And do not swear by your head, for you cannot make one hair white or black. Let what you say be simply "Yes" or "No"; anything more than this comes from evil.

In the history of the Christian church this passage has been interpreted in various ways. Some Christians interpret Jesus' words quite literally and refuse to swear an oath. Even in a court of law they will not swear an oath. They believe that they will violate the explicit command of

Jesus found in Matthew's passage. Should all Christians follow this interpretation and refuse to take such oaths?

Interpreting Jesus' words in this manner runs into serious problems. Four reasons will be examined in the reverse order of importance. First, such an interpretation would stand in sharp conflict with the explicit teachings of the Old Testament. In Leviticus 5:1, 19:12; Numbers 30:2–15; Deuteronomy 23:21–23; and Exodus 20:7 the legitimacy of such oaths is assumed. Taking an oath and not keeping it is rebuked! The relationship of the Old Testament Scriptures and covenant to the New Testament Scriptures and covenant comes to the forefront at this point. If the Old Testament is seen as contradicting the New Testament, a denial of all oath-taking is not a major problem. This will also be true if the Old Testament is viewed as a more primitive and crude revelation which is superseded by the New Testament.

If, however, both the Old and the New Testament are seen as witnessing to a common covenant of grace and are equally the Word of God, any interpretation which finds a contradiction between the Old Testament commands concerning oaths and the New Testament command to refrain from all oaths presents a serious problem! Regardless of whether a continuity is seen between the two Testaments (an emphasis found in "covenantal theology") or a discontinuity (an emphasis found in "dispensational theology"), the Christian should be most sensitive to rejecting any explicit Old Testament command too easily. The Old Testament is still part of the canon of Scripture. The least that can be said concerning a literal interpretation is that this passage's apparent conflict with explicit Old Testament teachings allows the believer to question whether this is a correct interpretation.

Second, a more serious objection to a literal interpretation of this passage is the fact that various oaths in the New Testament were made that are viewed positively. In Acts 2:30 and Hebrews 6:16–18, 7:20–22 positive mention is made of God's having sworn to emphasize the certainty of the promises He made. The apostle Paul also calls "God to witness" (2 Cor. 1:23), states "before God, I do not lie" (Gal. 1:20), and mentions that "God is my witness" (Phil. 1:8). Was Paul wrong to swear? It would appear that Paul did not interpret Jesus' teaching in this area literally. It might be argued that Paul was not aware of Jesus' teaching on this subject, but this is an assumption that cannot be proven, and does not solve the problem for the evangelical. It creates a greater one. A sharp conflict now exists between the New Testament teachings and Matthew 5:34–37; not just between the Old Testament and this passage. If any sort of doctrine of biblical infallibility is believed, it would seem reasonable to assume that Jesus' words in Matthew 5:34–37 should not be interpreted as an absolute and universal condemnation of all oath-taking.

The third reason why a literal interpretation of this passage should be rejected is because Matthew never interpreted these words in this manner. Before various antitheses in Matthew 5 ("You have heard that it was said . . . but I say. . . .") are interpreted as a rejection of the Old Testament teachings, it should be noted how they are introduced! Matthew 5:17 introduces these antitheses (of which this passage is one), by stating, "Think not that I have come to abolish the law and the prophets; I have come not to abolish them but to fulfil them." Matthew does not interpret these antitheses as contradicting the Old Testament teachings but as fulfilling them! A literal interpretation of this passage would appear to be destroying the law and the prophets rather than fulfilling them. Also, Matthew, as shall be seen shortly, records an instance where Jesus accepts being placed under an oath.

The fourth, and most important, reason why a universal and literal interpretation of Jesus' words cannot be accepted is that Jesus, himself, did not. At the trial of Jesus, during the questioning of the high priest, ". . . Jesus was silent" (Matt. 26:63). However, his silence ends when he is placed under an oath by the high priest who says, "I adjure you by the living God, tell us if you are the Christ, the Son of God" (Matt. 26:63). In accordance with Leviticus 5:1, Jesus realizes that he could not remain silent. To do so would be to violate the Old Testament command and to be judged guilty. (There was no possibility of "pleading the fifth amendment" in Israel.) Jesus accepts the validity of this oath and responds (Matt. 26:64).

It would appear that Jesus is reacting against the abuse of oaths common among certain elements in Jewish society. This seems clear from the context of this passage.[1] As a result he teaches by use of overstatement that the Christian's character is to be of such a quality that his word possesses absolute veracity. A simple yes or no is all that is needed. Those who follow "the way, and the truth, and the life" (John 14:6) only speak the truth! To ask such people to swear is unnecessary. Perhaps this teaching of Jesus means that when called upon in a court of law to "swear to tell the truth, the whole truth, and nothing but the truth, so help you God," the Christian can respond, "That is unnecessary, for Jesus has taught me to tell only the truth, but if it makes the court happy, 'I do!'"

"And forgive us our debts, As we also have forgiven our debtors" (Matt. 6:12)

In the Lord's Prayer (Matt. 6:9–13) the interpreter encounters a number of exegetical and theological problems. The exegetical issues include questions such as what is referred to by the expression "On earth as it is in heaven"? Does it refer to the last "Thou Petition" ("Thy will be done") or does it belong with all three "Thou Petitions" concerning the name, the kingdom, and the will of God? Another exegetical problem is the meaning of the term *daily*. Since this Greek term, *epiousion*, is found in only two places in Greek literature (in Matthew's and Luke's accounts of the Lord's Prayer), it is almost impossible to know exactly how this term should be translated.

Although these exegetical questions are troublesome, the theological issues in the Lord's Prayer pose greater problems. There are two main problems. The first problem involves the second "We Petition": "And forgive us our debts, As we also have forgiven our debtors." A minor issue involves the meaning of the term *debts*. This term was a common metaphor in Jesus' day for sins. This is most apparent in Luke's version of the Lord's Prayer. Luke 11:4 states, "and forgive us our sins, for we ourselves forgive every one who is indebted to us." It is clear by the interchange of these two terms that debts means sins. This is also evident from Matthew 18:32–35 and Luke 7:41–49.[2]

The major theological problem in this passage, however, is the issue of how God's forgiveness of the Christian is related to the Christian's forgiveness of others. It is clear that this is an important issue. Its importance is heightened by the fact that this petition is the only part of the Lord's Prayer in which the activity of the believer is involved! Only here is the person who prays the Lord's Prayer required to do anything.

Yet exactly how are Christian forgiveness and God's forgiveness related? The "as" in the petition should not be interpreted to mean "to the same degree" or "in the exact same manner." No believer wants his imperfect forgiving to limit the perfect forgiveness of God. And clearly no believer wants the extent of his forgiving to limit God's boundless forgiveness. No Christian praying this prayer is sinned against by his neighbor as greatly as he sins against God. The Christian clearly needs to be forgiven more by God than he needs to forgive others! Therefore, the term *as* cannot refer to a simple comparison of God's and the Christian's forgiveness.

Another issue that this petition raises involves the time frame of God's forgiveness. Some scholars suggest that the scene envisioned is the Great Day of Judgment and that the believer is seeking God's forgiveness in that day. It seems more reasonable, however, to see here a request for daily cleansing from sin and to interpret this along the lines of 1 John 1:9, "If we confess our sins, he is faithful and just, and will forgive our sins and cleanse us from all unrighteousness." This seems reasonable for at least two reasons. First, the person praying this prayer is a believer. He is redeemed. He is already justified and is a child and heir of God, because he addresses God as "Father."[3] He thus is assured of salvation in that day (Rom. 5:9).

Second, the Lord's Prayer was meant not only to be a pattern for prayer but also to be a prayer uttered continually by the followers of Jesus. The fact that this prayer would identify them as the disciples of Jesus, even as John the Baptist's disciples had such an identifying prayer, indicates that God is not being repeatedly asked to forgive in the Judgment Day, or in a sense to resave sinners.[4] Rather, Christians should seek continual restoration and cleansing in order to maintain a close Father-child relationship. An adopted son who offends his father needs to apologize and seek forgiveness not in order to remain adopted but to maintain a good relationship with his father. Similarly believers pray "forgive us our debts" in order to maintain a good relationship with their heavenly Father and not in order to be readopted, rejustified, or reforgiven.

The most significant issue in this petition involves the question of time. Which comes first: Christians forgiving others and as a result God forgiving them, or God forgiving believers and as a result Christians forgiving others? If the former is correct, does this imply a "works" type of righteousness? Is not faith the only necessity for divine forgiveness? The theological issue involved here is important and perplexing. In the Lord's Prayer it seems that God's forgiveness follows and is contingent on Christian forgiveness of others. The Christian can ask God to forgive because he has forgiven. Matthew 5:23–24 also implies this. It is necessary for a Christian to be reconciled to his neighbor before coming to God. Likewise, Luke 6:37 states, ". . . forgive, and you will be forgiven." Mark 11:25 teaches the same view. More important, Matthew 6:14, states, "For if you forgive men their trespasses, your heavenly Father also will forgive you."[5] It seems clear that Jesus teaches that divine forgiveness is dependent on and follows the believer forgiving others.

Yet, other biblical passages seem to teach that Christian forgiveness is simultaneous with or follows God's forgiveness. With regard to the former, the parallel account of the Lord's Prayer, Luke 11:4, reads, ". . . forgive us our sins, for we ourselves forgive every one who is indebted to us." Here Christian forgiveness is contemporaneous with God's forgiveness. On the other hand, Luke 7:47b states that God's forgiveness is followed by love and that love is a response to God's forgiveness. It is also clear from Luke 7:42–43 that one who is forgiven much, as a result, loves much. The idea that it is in response to God's grace of forgiveness that the Christian in turn forgives (or loves) is also found in Paul. Ephesians 4:32 and Colossians 3:13 both state that believers should forgive one another just as God in Christ forgave (note tense!) us.

At times it is necessary to forgive in order to be forgiven, to forgive because we are forgiven, to forgive as we are being forgiven! In the search for a proper and exact chronology, however, the central truth all these verses are shouting out must be kept in sight. That truth is the fact that being forgiven and forgiving are interdependent; they cannot be separated. At times the focus may be on one side and at other times on the other, but forgiving and being forgiven cannot be separated. Unforgiving means unforgiven (Matt. 6:15)!

At times the focus of Jesus may be directed to the initial experience of repentance and faith, where in humility the Christian seeks God's forgiveness and shows the necessary attitude for coming to God by forgiving debtors first. (To see in such humility and contrition, however, a works righteousness is absurd. A works righteousness does not seek mercy and grace, it demands it!) At other times the focus of Jesus or the biblical writer may not be on the initial act of repentance but on the outworking of that repentance and faith. Having tasted God's forgiveness, the believer now is both willing and able to forgive others.

Jesus and the writers of the New Testament appear to be less concerned with constructing a time scheme in this area than on proclaiming the necessary and integral tie between the experience of divine forgiveness and the practice of forgiving. Divine forgiveness results in and requires a willingness, on the believer's part, to forgive. To emphasize the former implies that the willingness to forgive others must follow being forgiven. To emphasize the latter implies that divine forgiveness follows the believer's forgiving. The parable of the unforgiving servant (Matt. 18:23–35) clearly teaches this interrelatedness. What appears like forgiveness which precedes forgiving (Matt. 18:27) disappears when forgiving does not follow (Matt. 18:32–35). These cannot be separated. Whether forgiveness occurs before, is simultaneous, or occurs after being forgiven is of little real consequence. The crucial concern is to realize there cannot be forgiveness without forgiving!

"And lead us not into temptation" (Matt. 6:13a)

The second theological problem in the Lord's Prayer is found in Matthew 6:13a: "And lead us not into temptation. . . ." Before dealing with the main difficulty found here, it may help to clarify a couple of minor issues. Some scholars define the term *temptation* as the eschatological "Temptation": "lead us not into the Great Temptation which is coming upon the earth." However, in Matthew 6:13a "temptation" lacks the article "the." (Even though an article is not necessary in a prepositional phrase to make the noun definite, its omission here is significant.) This indicates that the term *temptation* is used in a more general sense to refer to inward seductions. A good example of this is found in Matthew 26:41, Mark 14:38, and Luke 22:40. The same term is used, but it refers to the immediate temptation facing Peter and the disciples when Jesus is about to be betrayed.

The term *temptation* is used nine times in the Gospels, but it is never used to refer to the Temptation coming at the end of history. In fact, the expression is found twenty-one times in the New Testament and in only one instance it clearly refers to the Temptation (Rev. 3:10), although it may on two other instances as well (1 Peter 4:12; 2 Peter 2:9). Therefore it seems certain that in the Lord's Prayer Matthew is not referring to the eschatological Temptation that is coming at the end of history but to the daily temptation to sin that Christians face.

A second minor issue involves whether the term *temptation* is to be understood in an active ("lead me not into tempting God")[6] or in a passive sense ("let me not be tempted"). The active sense is unlikely since the parallel expression in the latter part of the verse is concerned with "being delivered." It is passive in meaning.

The main problem in this text is clear. Does God lead His children into temptation? Does He seek to cause us to sin? James 1:13, in sharp opposition to such a view, states, "Let no one say when he is tempted, 'I am tempted by God'; for God cannot be tempted with evil and he himself tempts no one." It furthermore is suggested that James 1:13 specifically was written in reaction to a misunderstanding of this petition in the Lord's Prayer. This cannot be demonstrated, but James 1:13 does highlight the problem with Matthew 6:13.

In the Lord's Prayer does the Christian plead with God in this petition not to bring temptation that can cause him to fall? If so, how is the believer to interpret all the great promises of divine deliverance and help during times of temptation? ". . . The Lord knows how to rescue the godly from trial . . ." (2 Peter 2:9). "No temptation has overtaken you that is not common to man. God is faithful, and he will not let you be tempted beyond your strength, but with the temptation will also provide the way of escape, that you may be able to endure it" (1 Cor. 10:13).[7] This interpretation of the text by which the Christian prays that God will not bring him into temptation stands in sharp contrast with the teachings of the rest of Scripture which emphasizes that God is the One who brings the believer through and out of temptation, not into it. (It is hypothetically possible that Jesus in this petition of the Lord's Prayer teaches something that stands in sharp conflict with the rest of the Bible, but before such a judgment is made it would be wise to see if such an interpretation is really demanded by this text.)

It should be noted that the term *temptation* can be understood both in a positive as well as in a negative sense. In James 1:13 "temptation" is clearly a negative reality, for it stems from lust and leads to sin (James 1:14–15). Yet in James 1:2, 12 and 1 Peter 1:6 "temptation" is seen as positive and as a means of growth and maturation of faith. To seek not to be tempted, in the negative sense of being enticed to sin, makes good sense. Temptation which seeks to mislead us into sin should be avoided. Yet temptation, in the sense of trial which leads to spiritual growth, should not be avoided but welcomed. "Count it all joy, my brethren, when you meet various trials [same Greek term!], for you know that the testing of your faith produces steadfastness" (James 1:2–3). If God leads the believer into temptation in the negative sense, a clear conflict with James 1:13 exists. According to this verse, God does not lead his children into this sort of temptation. As a result, to ask God not to lead and entice us into sin would be a very strange request, since God never does this! That kind of temptation fits the behavior of a god of

Greek mythology better than the God of our Bible. But should the believer, on the other hand, ask God not to permit him to experience those trials which produce steadfastness and patience? On the contrary, the believer should pray for perseverence in such trials, not preservation from them.

To resolve this petition's difficulty it seems necessary to define what "lead us not" actually means. It is probable that behind these words lies an Aramaic expression which, rather than asking God not to lead the Christian into temptation, is asking Him not to allow him to succumb to temptation. A helpful parallel to this is found in the Babylonian Talmud:

> Lead me not into the power of transgression,
> And bring me not into the power of sin,
> And not into the power of iniquity,
> And not into the power of temptation,
> And not into the power of anything shameful.[8]

In this example the pious Jew is not pleading with God not to lead him or bring him into these evils. He is asking God to keep him from succumbing to or committing them. In a similar way in the Lord's Prayer the Christian asks God to aid him so he will not succumb to temptation rather than asking God not to force him into experiencing such temptation. This petition is best understood as an idiomatic expression which can be translated, "Let us not succumb to temptation."

This understanding of this petition is supported not only by parallels in Jewish literature but also by the parallelism of the succeeding phrase. The phrase "but deliver us from evil," which formally is an example of antithetical parallelism, is, in meaning, an example of synonymous parallelism. This means that another way of expressing the meaning of "lead us not into temptation" is "deliver us from evil." In both petitions the believer is seeking God's aid in times of trial and the request is made for divine deliverance from trial or evil. If it is understood as a request that God not permit the believer to succumb to temptation, this petition in the Lord's Prayer no longer poses any major difficulty.

"If you forgive the sins of any" (John 20:23)

Another passage in the Gospels that raises numerous questions is John 20:23. Jesus tells the disciples after his resurrection, "If you forgive the sins of any, they are forgiven; if you retain the sins of any, they are retained." Two related passages are Matthew 16:19 and 18:18. Matthew 16:19 is addressed to Peter after his confession that Jesus is the Christ. It states, "I will give you the keys of the kingdom of heaven, and whatever you bind on earth shall be bound in heaven, and whatever you loose on earth shall be loosed in heaven." Matthew 18:18 appears to be addressed to the disciples (18:1), but it is evident that this entire chapter consists of teachings of Jesus addressed to the entire church. (See especially Matt. 18:2–4, 5–6, 7–9, etc.)

In Matthew 18:18 the church is given the same commission and responsibility that Peter receives in Matthew 16:19, "Truly, I say to you, whatever you bind on earth shall be bound in heaven, and whatever you loose on earth shall be loosed in heaven." In Matthew 18:18 it seems clear that this "binding" and "loosing" are associated with the forgiveness of sins. The verses preceding (vv. 15–17) and following (vv. 21–22) deal with the forgiveness of sins. Also, the concluding part of this chapter contains the parable of the unforgiving servant (vv. 23–35). It would seem, at least to Matthew, that the "binding" and "loosing" mentioned in Matthew 18:18 (and probably 16:19) are associated with the forgiveness of sins.

The primary problem that this passage raises is how the disciples and the church can "forgive" or "retain" the sins of others. Is this forgiveness effective or declaratory? Does the church have the authority to forgive the sins of others ("I, by the authority given me, forgive you of all your sins"), or is this the authority to declare and pronounce God's forgiveness of sins ("I, due to the promises of God's Word, declare that because you sincerely repent and confess your sins, God forgives all your sins")?

The latter is a better interpretation of this passage for at least three reasons. First, the Gospels make it clear that only God can forgive sins (Mark 2:5–7; Luke 7:48–49). Although the statement, "Who can forgive sins but God alone?" (Mark 2:7) comes from the lips of Jesus' opponents, it is evident that Jesus and the gospel writers all assume the truth of the statement and associate Jesus' authority to forgive sins with their understanding of Jesus' divine nature. God alone can forgive the sins of his people.[9]

Second, it is important to note how the early church fulfilled this commission. No examples of the early church effectively forgiving the sins of others can be found in Acts, but frequent examples of the proclamation of the forgiveness of sins are discovered in the preaching.[10] Acts reveals that the early church members understood this responsibility to mean that they were to proclaim the gospel of Jesus Christ. By doing this, they had the ability to bring about the forgiveness of sins when listeners responded in repentance and faith.

Finally, it should be observed that this passage speaks not only of the forgiveness of sins but of the "retaining" of sins as well! It is difficult to assume that God gives to his erring church, which is itself in continual need of repentance and renewal, the authority to effectively forgive or not forgive the sins of mankind for eternity. Surely, such authority lies only with God. Only God can know the true condition of the heart.

The means by which the church is to fulfill this commission is exemplified in 1 John 1:8–10. The writer declares how the forgiveness of sins can be received. To claim to have no sin (v. 8) means that the believer remains in sin; to confess sin (v. 9) results in God's faithful forgiveness of sins. The author of these words, by the proclamation of this truth, helps to bring about the forgiveness of sins to the repentant and the withholding of forgiveness to the unrepentant. It is also important to observe how the other gospel writers end their Gospels. Luke concludes with Jesus commanding his disciples that after the receiving of the Holy Spirit ". . . repentance and forgiveness of sins should be preached in his name to all nations, beginning from Jerusalem" (Luke 24:47). Matthew concludes with the commission to "Go therefore and make disciples of all nations, baptizing them in the name of the Father and of the Son and of the Holy Spirit" (Matt. 28:19).

Perhaps John 20:23, Luke 24:47, and Matthew 28:19 should be understood as different ways of expressing the same truth. With the coming of the Spirit, the disciples' proclamation of the gospel message would ". . . convince the world concerning sin and righteousness and judgment" (John 16:8). Through the preaching of the early church (and the preaching of today) others would believe (John 17:20) and receive the forgiveness of sins, or would not believe and be condemned (John 3:18). Baptism was frequently involved in this experience (Matt. 28:19–20). As the Book of Acts clearly reveals, baptism was intimately associated with the conversion experience in the early church. It generally occurred on the same day and often was seen as its culminating expression.

William Barclay seems to be on the right track when he states, "This sentence [John 20:23] does not mean that the power to forgive sins was ever entrusted to any man or to any men; it means that the power to proclaim that forgiveness was so entrusted; and it means that the power to warn that that forgiveness is not open to the impenitent was also entrusted to them."[11] The awesomeness of this commission should not be minimized. Each Christian has the opportunity to "forgive" or "retain" the sins of others! In the faithful proclamation of the gospel message the believer is a vital instrument in God's program of forgiveness and redemption!

Jesus' Teachings on Prayer (Mark 11:22–24; Matthew 7:7–8)

The Gospels contain numerous sayings of Jesus concerning prayer that are troublesome.

> And Jesus answered them, "Have faith in God. Truly, I say to you, whoever says to this mountain, 'Be taken up and cast into the sea,' and does not doubt in his heart, but believes that what he says will come to pass, it will be done for him. Therefore I tell you, whatever you ask in prayer, believe that you have received it, and it will be yours" (Mark 11:22–24).

> "Ask, and it will be given you; seek, and you will find; knock, and it will be opened to you. For every one who asks receives, and he who seeks finds, and to him who knocks it will be opened" (Matt. 7:7–8).

Matthew 18:19; Luke 11:5–13; John 14:13; 15:7, 16; 16:23–24, also are problematic. What makes these passages even more difficult is that some of them are not qualified or made conditional in any way. It is true that some of these promises do have qualifications: Mark 11:22–24 requires faith and not doubting but believing, as does its parallel, Matthew 21:21–22; Matthew 18:19 requires agreement in prayer between at least two people; John 15:7 requires abiding in Christ; John 14:13, 15:16, and 16:23–24 require asking in Jesus' name; but Matthew 7:7–8 and its parallel, Luke 11:5–13, are not conditional.

The problem created by these verses is evident. Christians through the centuries have at times asked and not received, sought and not found, knocked and not found it open. Furthermore, Christians have prayed in great unity numbering not just two or three (Matt. 18:19) but in the thousands, and have not been heard. Christians often have prayed with much faith, doubting nothing (Mark 11:22–24; Matt. 21:21–22), believing that they were indeed abiding in Christ (John 15:7), and praying in Jesus' name (John 14:13; 15:16; 16:23–24) and still have not had their prayers answered. How can this be explained?

The author quite vividly remembers being part of a prayer group and praying that a young man, who was listed as missing in action and presumed dead, would soon return home. We knew he was alive; we prayed persistently month after month in faith believing; and we prayed in Jesus' name. The young man never returned home. It might be argued that he is still alive and a prisoner of war. But these prayer sessions took place during the Korean War! Undoubtedly there have been similar prayers for the missing in action in World War II, World War I, and the Civil War.

One explanation for this apparent lack of answers to prayer is to raise additional qualifications. James 4:3 states, "You ask and do not receive, because you ask wrongly, to spend it on your passions." Are we to assume that Jesus' hearers would have known James 4:3 and added this and all the other biblical qualifications to the teachings of Jesus on prayer? Another rationalization for unanswered prayer is to say that all prayers are answered; God answers them with a "yes," a "no," or a "wait." This explanation appears to play with words and does not explain the serious problem of Christians who ask and do not receive. Furthermore Matthew 7:7–8 does not appear to allow "no" as an answer to prayer.

Another explanation is to say that the purpose of prayer

is not to receive things from God but to change; to become a different kind of person. There is an element of truth in this argument. Prayer is not synonymous with request or petition. Prayer does involve adoration, worship, and confession! The prayer Jesus taught, the Lord's Prayer, teaches this clearly. The problem lies in the fact that Jesus bids us to ask in order to receive. Prayer is not simply petition, but it does include it! Prayer does change the person praying, but it also, according to Jesus, changes "things." The fact cannot be evaded that Jesus encourages his followers to pray to the Father in his name in order to have their prayers and petitions answered.

Perhaps a more satisfying explanation of these verses is to be found in one of the methods Jesus uses in his teaching. This is a method every teacher uses: exaggeration or overstatement. When the use of qualifiers weakens the point being made or makes it more confusing, or when seeking to emphasize a point, exaggeration often is used. A parent utilizes overstatement when he tells his child, "Tell Daddy what you want for Christmas, and he will get whatever you want." Daddy will not get just anything for his child. There are things that could hurt him physically or impair his mental-moral-emotional-spiritual growth. The statement can be qualified: "Of course, Daddy must be able to afford it; he must believe that it will not be dangerous to your health; he must believe that it will not harm your developing sense of values, etc." But, this would only confuse the child and weaken the point. The point, that Daddy loves to give good things to his child, is brought home forceably by means of the exaggeration.

Jesus uses exaggeration or overstatement in his teaching, although the degree to which he uses these techniques may be debated. Luke 14:26; Matthew 5:23–24, 29–30; 7:1; and 10:34 demonstrate that Jesus frequently uses overstatement to drive home forcefully his point. Jesus' statements on prayer should be understood in this vein. Jesus wants his followers to know that the Father delights in answering the requests of his children. He, in effect, says, "Tell *Abba* (literally "Daddy") what you want and he will grant it that your joy might overflow." Although Jesus did not expect his listeners to know James 4:3, or similar verses in the New Testament, he did expect them to assume that such qualifiers would be understood.

In conclusion, Jesus' promises on prayer should be interpreted as broad general statements meant to emphasize God's readiness and desire to hear and answer the prayers of his people. Built into these statements is the understanding that believers should pray only for those things that will be good for their well-being, or, what will be in accord with God's will. At times believers may not even know for what or how they should actually pray (Rom. 8:26). In so praying they know that when they ask, they shall receive.

The Parable of the Unjust Steward (Luke 16:1–8)

He also said to the disciples, "There was a rich man who had a steward, and charges were brought to him that this man was wasting his goods. And he called him and said to him, 'What is this that I hear about you? Turn in the account of your stewardship, for you can no longer be steward.' And the steward said to himself, 'What shall I do, since my master is taking the stewardship away from me? I am not strong enough to dig, and I am ashamed to beg. I have decided what to do, so that people may receive me into their houses when I am put out of the stewardship.' So, summoning his master's debtors one by one, he said to the first, 'How much do you owe my master?' He said, 'A hundred measures of oil.' And he said to him, 'Take your bill, and sit down quickly and write fifty.' Then he said to another, 'And how much do you owe?' He said, 'A hundred measures of wheat.' He said to him, 'Take your bill, and write eighty.' The master commended the dishonest steward for his shrewdness; for the sons of this world are more shrewd in dealing with their own generation than the sons of light."

Perhaps the one parable of Jesus that causes the greatest difficulty is the parable of the unjust steward in Luke 16:1–8. Undoubtedly the original hearers, and believers today, are surprised by the conclusion: "The master commended the dishonest steward for his shrewdness . . ." (Luke 16:8). The reader expects the master to rebuke, judge, condemn, punish, or damn the steward for his dishonesty. But the parable takes an unexpected twist, and he not only does not condemn him but commends the scoundrel. How can Jesus in this parable commend such a person? Does this not reward and encourage dishonesty?

This is not the only parable in which people of questionable character and morality are commended. In the parable of the hidden treasure (Matt. 13:44) the man, whose behavior serves as an example, obtains the treasure by less than exemplary means. He may not have swindled or defrauded to obtain the land with its treasure, but it is impossible to hold him up as an example of one who practices the Golden Rule (Matt. 7:12). Furthermore, in the parable of the wise and foolish maidens (Matt. 25:1–13) the Christian is taught to emulate the wise maidens who did not share their oil with those who had need. Are Christians to follow this kind of an example or are they to "Give to him who begs from you, and do not refuse him who would borrow from you" (Matt. 5:42)?

The problem these parables raise is due to a misunderstanding of the purpose and function of parables. In the history of the church parables have frequently been understood as allegories in which each detail has meaning and significance. An example would be the parable of the good Samaritan (Luke 10:30–35). The following analogies are drawn:

Man	=	Adam
Jerusalem	=	Paradise
Jericho	=	This world
Robbers	=	The Devil and his angels
Wounds	=	Disobedience or sins
Priest	=	Law
Levite	=	Prophets
Good Samaritan	=	Christ
Beast	=	The body of Christ
Inn	=	Church
Two Denarii	=	Two commandments of love
Innkeeper	=	Angels in charge of church
Return of Good Samaritan	=	Second coming of Christ

Since the turn of this century it is clear that parables are not allegories. Details are important in allegories. However, a parable usually contains one basic point of comparison. The details are generally unimportant and should not be pressed for meaning. As a result, in the parable of the good Samaritan, if the man were going up from Jericho or if it were three denarii rather than two, the point of the parable would not change at all. A parable then is a basic metaphor in which an analogy is presented. "A" (for example, the kingdom of God) is likened to "B" (for example, a grain of mustard seed). The very nature of any analogy guarantees that the analogy will eventually break down if pressed beyond the basic point of comparison. The reason for this is that "A" can only be identical in all areas of comparison with itself. In other words, the kingdom of God is identical in all points only with the kingdom of God, or with itself. It is similar to something else (a grain of mustard seed, leaven which a woman took, or a merchant in search of pearls) only in its basic point of comparison.

Another example is to say that "God is like. . . ." No analogy can be used for God if the analogy must correspond to God in all its details, for no one or nothing is Infinite, Omniscient, Omnipresent, or Omnipotent but God. Yet it can be said that God is like a father, who . . . , if the one basic comparison that the analogy is seeking to make can be accepted.

In interpreting any analogy, the interpreter should content himself with the basic point of comparison being made. If the details are not pressed in the parable of the unjust steward, the problem that the parable causes will disappear. What is the point of comparison Jesus is making in the parable? What does he commend? It is not the dishonesty of the steward but his shrewdness: his cleverness and skill for self-preservation. He is commended for preparing himself for judgment coming on him from his master. After being fired, he still has "friends" who owe him favors and will receive him into their houses when he is put out of his stewardship.

This point of comparison was surely applicable to Jesus' audience. Jesus' message to "Repent, for the kingdom of God is at hand" encouraged believers to be prudent and prepare themselves. Also, knowing that ". . . it is appointed for men to die once, and after that comes judgment" (Heb. 9:27), should not Christians today be prudent and prepare for this accounting of stewardship? How to prepare for this is suggested, in part, by Luke 16:9. It is by the judicious use of possessions ("unrighteous mammon"). The parable therefore does not exhort believers to be cunning thieves but to be at least as shrewd or prudent as the scoundrel in the parable and make ready for that great day in which an account must be rendered to God.[12]

"Let him who has no sword . . . buy one" (Luke 22:36)

Luke 22:36 contains a saying of Jesus which seems to be out of character with the tenor of Jesus' teachings elsewhere. Jesus says, "But now, let him who has a purse take it, and likewise a bag. And let him who has no sword sell his mantle and buy one." This passage can be translated a couple of ways: (1) Let the person who has a purse and wallet take them and buy a sword, and let the person who does not have them sell his cloak and buy a sword; or (2) Let the person who has a sword take his purse or wallet; and let the person who does not have a sword sell his cloak and buy one. With each interpretation, however, the difficulty remains.

There have been numerous attempts to interpret this saying and others such as Matthew 10:34: "Do not think that I have come to bring peace on earth; I have not come to bring peace, but a sword." to indicate that Jesus was a political revolutionary: a zealot or at least a zealot sympathizer.[13]

Such an interpretation is clearly impossible for several reasons. First, there are many other passages in which Jesus' words are clearly not non-revolutionary but are anti-revolutionary.[14] Second, Jesus' frequent association with publicans (tax collectors) would be impossible for anyone holding zealot sympathies. The zealots hated tax collectors and considered them traitors because they collected taxes for the Roman oppressors. Furthermore, to have a disciple who was a tax collector would be inconceivable for a zealot sympathizer.

In Matthew 10:34 the "sword" Jesus comes to bring has nothing to do in the context with politics but speaks of the family division and strife that he frequently brings.

For I have come to set a man against his father, and a
daughter against her ˻ mother, and a daughter-in-law
against her mother-in-law; and a man's foes will be those
of his own household (Matt. 10:35–36).

Finally, if two swords are "enough" (Luke 22:38), Jesus
did not intend to establish a military revolution. Two swords
are clearly not "enough" against the legions of Rome!

Since Luke 22:36 does not promote a revolutionary
outlook, a reasonable interpretation of this passage must
be found. It is clear that any literal interpretation of the
passage is incorrect. When the disciples think literally of
swords and respond, "Look, Lord, here are two swords,"
Jesus rebukes them with "It is enough." Perhaps the best
interpretation is to see these words as an idiomatic way of
stopping a conversation that is on the wrong track by
saying, "That is enough [of such foolish talk]." An example of this can be found in Deuteronomy 3:26 where, in
the LXX, the Lord puts a stop to Moses' conversation by
stating, "Let it suffice you; speak no more to me of this
matter." In the context of Luke 22:36, the disciples have
completely misunderstood Jesus' words by taking them
literally. Jesus simply ends the conversation.

What then is Jesus seeking to teach by this saying on
buying a sword? If the context is noted, it can be seen that
in the preceding verse Jesus reminds his disciples that
earlier in his ministry when he sent them out to preach
they had no need for purse or bag or sandals. They were
completely taken care of by the cordial reception of their
audience. This took place during the height of Jesus'
popularity and they experienced great hospitality from the
people.[15] But now the situation has changed. Jesus will
soon be crucified. Instead of hospitality, the disciples can
expect hostility and persecution. They need to prepare for
this new situation by providing themselves with a purse
and a bag. The need for a sword can be understood as a
metaphorical way of describing the hardship and struggle

of the "war" they are to fight for the cause of Christ. This "war" will at times involve persecution and perhaps martyrdom.[16] At times the struggle will involve a "war" against sin and temptation. Jesus' use of the sword metaphor is to prepare the disciples to enter this battle with dedication, fully armed. The use of other related metaphors of war may lend support to this interpretation.[17]

Rather than interpreting this saying literally, which is impossible in the light of Jesus' life and teachings elsewhere, perhaps it is best to interpret it as a metaphor describing the war his followers are now involved in.[18]

> The saying can be regarded only grimly ironical, expressing the intensity of the opposition which Jesus and the disciples will experience, endangering their very lives. They are summoned to a faith and courage which is prepared to go to the limit.[19]

"You are Peter, and on this rock I will build my church"(Matt. 16:18)

Matthew 16:18 has been a continual battlefield for commentators. It states "And I tell you, you are Peter, and on this rock I will build my church, and the powers of death shall not prevail against it." The importance of this verse is evident. It serves as the theological cornerstone for the establishment of the papacy in Roman Catholic theology. The traditional Catholic interpretation of this verse is that the rock upon which Christ will build the church is Peter, who will serve as Christ's vicar on the earth. This role subsequently passed to succeeding bishops who serve as Christ's vicar or pope.

The Protestant interpretation argues that the rock Jesus refers to is not Peter but rather Peter's confession: that Jesus is the Christ. According to this view, Christ is the foundation of the church. No other foundation exists (1 Cor. 3:11). He alone possesses the keys of death and

Hades (Rev. 1:18). For the Roman Catholic exegete, the issue is clear. The rock on which Jesus will build the church must be the same rock Jesus refers to earlier in the verse: Peter.

Without discussing immediately the correctness or incorrectness of these interpretations, it may be profitable to consider the danger of approaching the Scriptures with preconceived ideas on what a text can or cannot say. Regardless of which interpretation is correct, it is frightening that the meaning of the text no longer serves as a final authority. On the contrary, it is the present theology that predetermines what the text means and that serves as a final authority! Hopefully, theology is derived from the Scriptures. But the believer continually must be aware of which determines which and never allow any theological formulations to supersede the Scriptures. The final authority in all religious matters is the Scriptures. Theology is "final" only to the degree that it accurately understands and interprets the meaning of the Scriptures. For a Protestant or a Roman Catholic to predetermine what Matthew 16:18 can or cannot mean is to place a particular theology above the Scriptures.

This passage, in the Greek translation, contains a pun: a play on the words *Peter* (*petros* in Greek) and *rock* (*petra* in Greek). Some commentators seek to minimize the importance of the pun by pointing out that these words are not identical. "Peter" is a masculine noun whereas "rock" is a feminine noun. Two considerations argue against this. First, the difference between the two is due to the fact that the word *rock* is always feminine in Greek, whereas Peter's name must be masculine. Second, in Aramaic, which Jesus spoke, there would be no difference in the two words. The word used by Jesus for *Peter* and for *rock* would be the same: *Cephas.*

Without claiming that the following interpretation is inerrant, perhaps the best interpretation of the word *rock* is that it refers to Peter. This interpretation alone does justice to the play on words found in the verse. Yet what did Jesus mean by this? How does the New Testament portray Peter's fulfillment of this role? The New Testament does not present an infallible Peter.[20] Peter is used by God to preach to the Jews at Pentecost (Acts 2) and to Cornelius at the "Gentile Pentecost" (Acts 10), and he provided the leadership for the early church. It is in his role as apostle and in his proclamation of the gospel that Peter serves as a foundation for the church. It is in a similar manner that all the early apostles serve as a "foundation" on which the church is built, although Jesus Christ is the cornerstone (Eph. 2:20). Peter is the "rock" of Matthew 16:18 in the sense that without the apostles (and Peter was the leader at the beginning) there would be no church.

According to this understanding both traditional interpretations of this passage are right in one sense and wrong in another. The Roman Catholic view is correct in that the pun demands that the rock refer to Peter, but is incorrect in building a papal edifice based on this verse. The traditional Protestant interpretation is incorrect in ignoring the pun and saying that the rock refers to Peter's confession, but it is certainly correct in realizing that the only ultimate foundation on which the church can be built is Jesus Christ. There is no need for Protestants to minimize the important role our Lord gave to the apostle Peter as leader of the apostles. This man was one of the great gifts God gave for the establishment of His church (Eph. 2:20). Protestants and Roman Catholics alike can give God thanks for his leadership.

The Parable of the Rich Man and Lazarus (Luke 16:19–31)

There was a rich man, who was clothed in purple and fine linen and who feasted sumptuously every day. And at his gate lay a poor man named Lazarus, full of sores, who desired to be fed with what fell from the rich man's table;

moreover the dogs came and licked his sores. The poor man died and was carried by the angels to Abraham's bosom. The rich man also died and was buried; and in Hades, being in torment, he lifted up his eyes, and saw Abraham far off and Lazarus in his bosom. And he called out, "Father Abraham, have mercy upon me, and send Lazarus to dip the end of his finger in water and cool my tongue; for I am in anguish in this flame." But Abraham said, "Son, remember that you in your lifetime received your good things, and Lazarus in like manner evil things; but now he is comforted here, and you are in anguish. And besides all this, between us and you a great chasm has been fixed, in order that those who would pass from here to you may not be able, and none may cross from there to us." And he said, "Then I beg you, father, to send him to my father's house, for I have five brothers, so that he may warn them, lest they also come into this place of torment." But Abraham said, "They have Moses and the prophets; let them hear them." And he said, "No, father Abraham; but if someone goes to them from the dead, they will repent." He said to him, "If they do not hear Moses and the prophets, neither will they be convinced if some one should rise from the dead."

The account of Lazarus and the rich man, Luke 16:19–31, is prone to serious misinterpretation. There is considerable debate whether this passage is to be interpreted as a true story or as a parable. There are two arguments in favor of it being a true story of an actual rich man and a poor man named Lazarus. First, the story is not called a parable nor is it introduced like many parables ("the kingdom of God is like"; or "the kingdom of God can be compared to"). This is not a weighty argument. Many of the most famous parables also are not explicitly called parables nor introduced by a phrase such as "the kingdom of heaven is like. . . ."[21] But the strongest argument in favor of the non-parabolic nature of this passage is the fact that the poor man is explicitly given a name: Lazarus. No other parable gives a character a specific name!

There are at least two strong reasons in favor of interpreting this passage as a parable. First, there are details in
the account which do not seem to conform with other
Scriptural teachings concerning life after death. This
would not be a problem in the context of a parable. It
would be if this were an historical account. The strongest
and most conclusive argument in favor of a parable is the
way in which the story is introduced. "There was a
[certain—*tis* in Greek] rich man, who. . . ." The Gospel of
Luke uses this introduction only to introduce various
parables. [22] It would seem best to interpret Luke 16:19–31
as a parable rather than as an historical story; most
scholars do.

The parable is unusual in that, in Luke, it is a two-part
parable similar to the parable of the gracious father (or the
prodigal son) in Luke 15:11–32. Interpreters frequently
place the emphasis on the first half of both parables. The
point of the parable of the rich man and Lazarus would be
the reversal of fortune in the hereafter. Luke 15:11–32
would teach about the love of God toward the outcasts of
society.

Yet the emphasis in a parable comes at the end! In
parabolic interpretation this technique is termed "the rule
of end stress": at the end of a parable the main stress or
emphasis should be sought. The main two characters in
the parable of the gracious father therefore are not the
father (God) and the prodigal (the publicans and sinners),
but the father (God) and the older brother (the Pharisees
and scribes). This parable is directed to older brothers. Luke
15:2–3 states, "And the Pharisees and the scribes murmured, saying, 'This man receives sinners and eats with
them.' So he told them this parable. . . ." The parable of
the lost sheep, the parable of the lost coin, and the parable
of the gracious father follow. Jesus addresses these three
parables to the Pharisees and scribes who protest his offer
of divine forgiveness to the publicans and sinners, to
"prodigals." The emphasis of the parable comes at the end

where the Pharisaic attitude of the older brother toward the prodigal (the publicans and sinners) is rebuked by Jesus.

Similarly, the emphasis of the parable in Luke 16:19–31 comes at the end. It is true that there will be a reversal of roles in the hereafter: "So the last will be first, and the first last" (Matt. 20:16). But the emphasis in Luke's parable falls on the rejection by Jesus of a sign! Jesus says, "This generation is an evil generation; it seeks a sign, but no sign shall be given to it except the sign of Jonah" (11:29). Although the sign of one coming back from the dead would not force people to believe, if their hearts were open Moses and the prophets (and the life and teachings of Jesus) would suffice. On the other hand, if their hearts were closed, nothing would persuade them to believe. The resurrection of Jesus did not bring about a mass conversion to him. It is helpful to note the account of the resurrection of Lazarus (note the name!) in John 11–12 and the response of those whose hearts were closed.

> When the great crowd of the Jews learned that he was there, they came, not only on account of Jesus but also to see Lazarus, whom he had raised from the dead. So the chief priests planned to put Lazarus also to death, because on account of him many of the Jews were going away and believing in Jesus (John 12:9–11).

The greatest hindrance to faith in Jesus lies not in the mind's lack of knowledge, but in the heart's unwillingness to repent!

Another rule for interpreting parables is to realize that parables are not allegories. Parables teach one main point and the details should not be pressed for meaning. This does not mean that in some parables the details are not important. Clearly some parables such as the parable of the soils (Mark 4:3–9) and the parable of the evil tenants (Mark 12:1–11) contain details that are significant and that must be interpreted. In general, most parables, like any metaphor or simile, contain one main point of comparison. If their details are pressed, the analogy sooner or later breaks down. In the parable under discussion it is especially important not to press some of the details. If this is done an incorrect picture of the hereafter will be gained. Jesus was not seeking to teach his audience that heaven can be seen from hell (Luke 16:23). Nor was he teaching that the damned in hell can speak to Abraham in heaven (v. 24). It is not certain if being thirsty and in flames (v. 24) are literal in Jesus' understanding of life after death or are simply metaphors to describe the horrors of judgment and the final state for the unrighteous.

If the specific details in this parable are not pressed and its main point is studied, can our Lord's beliefs concerning life after death be understood? It would appear that this is possible. Jesus must have believed in certain realities pictured in this parable or the entire parable would be meaningless. In his parables he uses real-life, down-to-earth examples and analogies to make his points. It is true that the parables often include exaggeration (not all fathers are like the gracious father of the prodigal son), but Jesus' parables are not fables! They always portray real-life situations even when they contain unusual features.

Although certain aspects in the portrayal of the life to come may be exaggerated, the general portrayal of that life must generally agree with what Jesus believes. Jesus believes in life after death as evidenced in this parable and his teachings elsewhere.[23] Jesus clearly agrees with the Pharisees, not the Sadducees in this instance. The Pharisees believe in life after death; in particular in the resurrection of the body. The Sadducees did not believe in either.[24] The apostle Paul also gives clear evidence of the same belief of a conscious individual existence after death;[25] as does Peter (1 Peter 1:3–5; 4:6); the writer of Revelation (7:9–17; 19:1–21:27; 22:1–5); John (5:25–29); and the writer of Hebrews (12:22–23).

Additional aspects of Jesus' belief in the hereafter also can be obtained from the parable. He believes that both righteous and unrighteous exist in a conscious state of awareness after death and that for the former this is a state of great bliss (Luke 16:22, 25) and for the latter a place of great torment (vv. 24–25, 28). The state of the righteous (Lazarus) and the unrighteous (the rich man) as unchangeable seems to be suggested by Jesus (v. 26). Any other attempts to ascertain more of Jesus' (and Luke's) beliefs concerning life after death from this parable would probably be unwarranted.

In summarizing Jesus' teaching in this parable it must again be stressed that pressing the various details of the parable should be avoided. The main emphasis should be placed on the particular point Jesus makes. That point involves Jesus' rejection of the demand for a sign by his opponents. No amount of signs can produce faith if the heart is hard toward God. Even his own resurrection, and that of a different Lazarus in John 11, could not produce faith in the hearts of his opponents. When there is present a desire to know and a willingness to obey (John 7:17), then the Scriptures are sufficient for faith. Through the ministry of the Spirit, the truth of Scriptures is impressed in the minds of those whose hearts are open to the Gospel and faith results. Luke hoped this would result from Theophilus' reading of his Gospel (Luke 1:1–4) just as it did through the written Word and its interpretation to the Ethiopian eunuch (Acts 8:26-39) and through the proclamation and interpretation of the Word to the two disciples on the way to Emmaus (Luke 24:13–35).

"No one has ascended into heaven but he who descended" (John 3:13)

One passage in the Gospel of John that causes numerous interpretation problems is John 3:13. Jesus says to

Nicodemus "No one has ascended into heaven but he who descended from heaven, the Son of man." One major question frequently raised is: Does not the statement *"No one* has ascended into heaven but . . . the Son of man" conflict with the well-known fact that both Enoch (Gen. 5:24) and Elijah (2 Kings 2:1–12) ascended into heaven? Did Jesus or John err here? Another question that causes difficulty is: How could Jesus say "No one has ascended into heaven but he who descend*ed* [note tense!] . . ." since he had not yet ascended into heaven?

It should be noted that the first question tends to lose sight of the context of this verse. In John 3:12 Jesus states, "If I have told you earthly things and you do not believe, how can you believe if I tell you heavenly things?" The immediate context deals with the subject of divine revelation and the source of such revelation. If Nicodemus cannot understand and believe the more basic spiritual truths portrayed in the earthly analogies of birth and wind (the "earthly things") how can Jesus teach him more advanced spiritual truths (the "heavenly things")?[26] Where does such truth come from? Where does one learn of such heavenly things?

The human inability to ascertain divine truth, or the need for divine revelation, is not only a basic evangelical belief but was and is a basic belief of Judaism as well. The inability to bring down revelation from heaven is strongly attested to in the Old Testament as well as in the other Jewish literature.

> For this commandment which I command you this day is not too hard for you, neither is it far off. It is not in heaven, that you should say, "Who will go up for us to heaven, and bring it to us, that we may hear it and do it?" Neither is it beyond the sea, that you should say, "Who will go over the sea for us, and bring it to us, that we may hear it and do it?" But the word is very near you; it is in your mouth and in your heart, so that you can do it (Deut. 30:11–14).[27]

Your understanding has utterly failed regarding this world, and do you think you can comprehend the way of the Most High? (2 Esdras/4 Ezra 4:2)

We can hardly guess at what is on earth, and what is at hand we find with labor; but who has traced out what is in the heavens? (Wisdom of Solomon 9:16)

The Emperor also said to Rabban Gamaliel: "I know what your God is doing, and where He is seated." Rabban Gamaliel became overcome and sighed, and on being asked the reason, answered, "I have a son in one of the cities of the sea, and I yearn for him. Pray tell me about him." "Do I then know where he is," he [the Emperor] replied. "You do not know what is on earth, and yet (claim to) know what is in heaven!" he retorted (Sanhedrin 39a).

For the Judeo-Christian tradition, revelation, like salvation, is not a human achievement from below but a gift of God's grace from above!

This inability to attain the knowledge of God and his will by human effort is expressed idiomatically by the inability to ascend to heaven to acquire such truth. Whatever the original source for the expression (and it may be Deuteronomy 30:12), its frequent occurrence in Jewish literature reveals that it was a common idiom in Judaism.

Who has ascended to heaven and come down? (Prov. 30:4a)

. . . perhaps you would have said to me, "I never went down into the deep, not as yet into hell, neither did I ever ascend into heaven" (2 Esdras/4 Ezra 4:8).

Who has gone up into heaven, and taken her [wisdom], and brought her down from the clouds? (Baruch 3:29)

It is apparent that the thought in John 3:13 is a common expression: that no one has ascended into heaven in order

to bring down the truth of God's nature and will. Enoch
and Elijah were not exceptions. Their ascensions were of a
totally different nature. They ascended but did not descend and the idiom always refers to, or at least implies,
descending or returning to bring back knowledge of God.
Enoch's and Elijah's ascension clearly had nothing to do
with bringing divine revelation to mankind. (It should be
assumed that both Jesus and John knew the Old Testament
too well to make a simple historical blunder of this sort
and that it is probable that they did not see Enoch or Elijah
as exceptions to their statement.)

The only exception to the idiom that no one has
ascended into heaven is, of course, Jesus, the Son of man,
who descended from heaven. This then brings us to our
second major difficulty with this passage. How can Jesus
state that the Son of man ascended into heaven since his
ascension had not yet taken place. His descension is not a
problem. When he said these words he had already
descended. The Word became flesh! But the ascension was
in the future.

There have been numerous attempts to explain this
difficulty:

1. Some scholars suggest that this reference speaks of
   Jesus' future ascension by way of anticipation. In
   other words, the passage uses a futuristic or dramatic
   aorist in which the past tense is used because of the
   certainty of the event which is about to take place.
   This is a possible use of the aorist tense, but is not a
   likely explanation.
2. One writer suggests that the term *ascended* should be
   understood metaphorically as referring to Jesus' experience at his baptism when he directly communed
   ("ascended") with God. This explanation presents
   two problems. First, it conflicts with the fact that the
   term *descended* in this passage is not to be understood

metaphorically. Second, no reader of John would have interpreted the term *ascended* in this way. For the early readers the natural reading of ascended would have been perfectly acceptable since Jesus indeed ascended into heaven.

3. Another possibility is that John 3:13 is not spoken by Jesus but is an interpretive comment by the Evangelist. The statement was true when he wrote. By then Jesus had ascended into heaven. In support of this interpretation is the well-known fact that it is impossible to know exactly where Jesus' words in John 3 end and the words of the Evangelist begin. If a red-letter edition of John were composed and red letters were used to indicate the words of Jesus, where would the red end? Would it end at verse 21, or 13? This question is impossible to answer. Furthermore, even if some of the verses after verse 13 should be red, this does not mean that verse 13 should not be interpreted as a parenthetical comment by the Evangelist and should therefore be in black!

4. A final possibility is that John 3:13 is an actual saying of Jesus (it should be colored in red) and that Jesus uses the future tense "shall ascend" because he had not yet ascended. John changed the tense "shall ascend" to "ascended" because when he wrote his Gospel Jesus had ascended into heaven. In other words, John changed the future tense of Jesus' saying to the past tense because the passage had been future for Jesus and is now past for John's readers. One of the last two explanations is probably correct.

"But of that day . . . no one knows . . . [not even] the Son" (Mark 13:32)

One of the most important christological passages in the Gospels is Mark 13:32. This passage also presents problems for many Christians. At the end of the Olivet discourse Jesus states: "But of that day or that hour no one knows, not even the angels in heaven, nor the Son, but only the Father." The importance of this verse is evident for two reasons. First, Jesus clearly distinguishes between himself as the Son and others. He makes a clear distinction between "no one" (mankind), the angels, and himself. He is the Son! Jesus states that he understood his Sonship as distinct and unique from his disciples and us. Others might become "sons of God" through faith and the receiving of the Spirit (Rom. 8:14; Gal. 3:26), but he was the Son of God by his very nature.[28] This passage is important because it demonstrates Jesus' self-understanding as the unique Son of God. Second, the passage is important because of its strong claim to authenticity. Even for skeptics who question whether the words found in the Gospels actually came from the lips of Jesus, this passage's authenticity is hard to deny. Who in the early church would create a saying in which the Son of God claims to be ignorant, and then place it on the lips of Jesus? The Apocryphal Gospels written in the second, third, and fourth centuries A.D. heighten the divine nature and miraculous ministry of Jesus to an absurd degree. (In these works the child Jesus commands trees to bend down, makes sparrows out of clay, stretches wood for Joseph, strikes people dead because they bump into him, etc.) To create a saying in which Jesus is ignorant of anything goes against this tendency to emphasize the divine nature of the Son of God at the expense of his humanity. Mark 13:32 must be an authentic saying of Jesus.

Another problem with this verse, which should assure its authenticity, is the question of how the Son of God, who was "very God of very God" according to the creeds and possessed unique knowledge,[29] could not have known the "day or that hour." One type of reasoning that raises this question is deductive logic:

Jesus was (and is) God.

As God, he must have possessed the attributes of God.

One of the attributes of God is omniscience.

Therefore Jesus, as God, possessed omniscience; he knew all things. This reasoning makes the passage difficult. The difficulty does not lie in the grammar of the passage and is not exegetical. On the contrary, the text can be interpreted only as a statement that the Son knows neither the day nor the hour of his return. The problem is clearly a theological one. How can this passage be interpreted to fit a particular theological understanding of the nature of Jesus' deity?

One solution is to say that Jesus may not know the exact day or hour but that he certainly knows the year or the month. This solution must be rejected. Any ignorance, whether the day or the hour or the minute or second, cannot be accepted if Jesus as the Son of God possessed divine omniscience during his ministry. Another attempted explanation is that in his human nature Jesus of Nazareth did not know the exact day or hour but that in his divine nature as the Son of God he does. Jesus is speaking with regard to his human nature in this passage. The problem with this solution is that Jesus is speaking of himself as the Son. It is as the unique Son of God, distinct from all others, that he does not know!

In this instance, rather than trying to make the passage fit a theological understanding of the divine nature of Jesus, a theological understanding of the divine nature of Jesus should fit the text! The text is clear. Jesus as the Son did not know the exact time of the end. No theological formulation of the natures of the Son of God possesses the authority that our text of Scripture possesses! Such formulations are not infallible but must always be judged by the Scripture. We need to make theological formulations fit Mark 13:32; not the reverse. Furthermore, no theological formulation about the natures of the Son of God is as simple to understand or as clear as this passage. The more complicated passages should be interpreted in the light of the clear and simple. In other words, more complicated theological summaries about the natures of the Son of God should be formulated in the light of clear and simple biblical statements.

In conclusion it may not be possible to know how Jesus could be "very God of very God" and not know the exact time of his return. It may not be possible to formulate exactly how both could be true, but the clear meaning of Mark 13:32 cannot be sacrificed to fit any formulation. Perhaps a clue for an understanding may be found in Philippians 2:6–11 which speaks of the emptying (kenosis) of the Son of God at the incarnation. However, the Son of God does not know when he will return, because he said so in Mark. Concerning the question of when the Lord will return, it does not require a great deal of humility for a Christian to say, "Just like Jesus I do not know exactly when the end will be." On the other hand, Jesus' words in this passage serve as a powerful rebuke of all who make such claims!

Notes

1. Note Matthew 5:34–37.
2. That the expression *debt* was a common term for sin in late, or post-biblical, Judaism is evident from the Targums. See their translations of Genesis 18:20–26; Exodus 32:31, 34:7; Numbers 14:18–19; and Isaiah 53:4, 12 where they use the Aramaic term for *debts* to translate "sins."
3. Cf. Romans 8:15–17; Galatians 4:4–7.
4. Cf. Luke 11:1.
5. Cf. Sirach 28:2: "Forgive your neighbor the wrong he has done, and then your sins will be pardoned when you pray."

6. Cf. Luke 4:12; Acts 5:9, 15:10; 1 Corinthians 10:9; etc.

7. Cf. Hebrews 2:18, 4:15, etc.

8. Berakoth 60b.

9. Cf. Exodus 34:6–7; Isaiah 43:25, 44:22, 55:7; Psalms 103:3, 104:4; etc.

10. Cf. Acts 2:38, 5:31, 8:22, 10:43, 13:38–39, 28:18, etc.

11. William Barclay, *The Gospel of John*, vol. II (Philadelphia: Westminster Press, 1956), p. 319.

12. Cf. Matthew 25:14–30; 2 Corinthians 5:10.

13. The most recent and serious attempt is S. G. F. Brandon, *Jesus and the Zealots* (New York: Scribners, 1967).

14. See Matthew 5:38–42, especially v. 39, 26:52; Luke 6:27–29.

15. Cf. Luke 10:4f.

16. Cf. the metaphor of the "cross" used in passages such as Mark 8:34.

17. Note: "war" (1 Tim. 1:18; 1 Cor. 9:7; 2 Cor. 10:4); "fight" (1 Tim. 6:12; 2 Tim. 4:7; cf. Heb. 11:34); "being a soldier" (2 Tim. 2:3–4; Phil. 2:25); and even "bearing a sword" (Eph. 6:17; cf. Heb. 4:12; Rev. 1:16; 2:12, 16).

18. For a similar view see John Calvin, *A Harmony of the Evangelists Matthew, Mark, and Luke*, ed., David W. and Thomas F. Torrance (Grand Rapids: Eerdmans, 1972), on Luke 22:36.

19. I. H. Marshall, *Luke* (Grand Rapids: Eerdmans, 1978), p. 823.

20. See Mark 14:26–31, 66–72; Galatians 2:11–21.

21. Compare the following parables in this regard: the wise and foolish servants (Matt. 24:45–51); the two debtors (Luke 7:41–43); the good Samaritan (Luke 10:30–35); the great supper (Luke 14:15–24); the gracious father (the prodigal son) (Luke 15:11–32); etc.

22. Luke 14:16—"A [certain—*tis*] man once gave . . ."; Luke 15:11—"There was a [certain—*tis*] man who had . . ."; Luke 16:1—"There was a [certain—*tis*] rich man who . . ."; Luke 19:12—"A [certain—*tis*] nobleman went . . ."; compare also Luke 18:2—"In a certain city there was a [certain—*tis*] judge who . . ."

23. Cf. Matthew 6:19–21; 7:21–23; 10:28; 13:24–30, 36–43, 47–50; 25:31–46; etc.

24. Cf. Acts 23:6–8.

25. Cf. Philippians 1:23—"to depart and be with Christ"; 1 Corinthians 15:12–57—"the mortal nature must put on immortality"; 1 Thessalonians 4:13–18—"and so we shall always be with the Lord"; 2 Corinthians 5:1–5—"if the earthly tent we live in is destroyed, we have a building from God, a house not made with hands, eternal in the heavens"; 2 Corinthians 5:8—away from the body means to be home with the Lord; 2 Thessalonians 1:9—the unrighteous "suffer the pun-

ishment of eternal destruction and exclusion from the presence of the Lord": Romans 2:5–11—"to those who by patience in well-doing seek for glory and honor and immortality, he will give eternal life"; 2 Timothy 4:6–8; etc.

26. Cf. Hebrews 5:11–14; 1 Corinthians 3:1–3.

27. Deuteronomy 29:29; Psalm 115:16.

28. Cf. Mark 1:1, 11; 3:11; 5:7; 9:7; 15:39; John 3:16; etc.

29. Cf. Mark 2:8; John 2:25, 5:16, 6:64; etc.

3

Difficult Actions of Jesus

Various actions of Jesus in the Gospels occasionally cause problems for the reader. In certain instances Jesus' actions seem inconsistent both with his actions and with his teachings elsewhere. Throughout the Gospels Jesus is portrayed as gently, loving, and kind. He is especially a friend to the poor and to the needy. However, several actions of Jesus, at first glance, appear cruel, harsh, and unkind.

Jesus' Cursing of the Fig Tree (Mark 11:12–14)

> On the following day, when they came from Bethany, he was hungry. And seeing in the distance a fig tree in leaf, he went to see if he could find anything on it. When he came to it, he found nothing but leaves, for it was not the season for figs. And he said to it, "May no one ever eat fruit from you again." And his disciples heard it.

The Gospels contain several instances in which Jesus appears to act in a way that seems out of character with his gracious and loving demeanor. Examples of this would be:

1. His destruction of the property of others in the case of the two thousand swine (Mark 5:11–13).

103

2. His apparent reluctance to heal the daughter of a
   Canaanite, or Gentile, woman (Mark 7:24–30).
3. His apparent unwillingness to permit a young man to
   honor his father by seeing that he receive a decent
   burial (Luke 9:59–60) or for another to bid farewell to
   his family (Luke 9:61–62).
4. His destruction or cursing of a fruitless fig tree (Mark
   11:12–14, 20–25).

In the latter instance, this action of Jesus is particularly
distasteful and a stumbling-block for many. One commen-
tator remarks that this is the least attractive narrative
about Jesus in the Gospels. It seems unworthy of him.
Others deny its historicity because they cannot conceive of
Jesus blasting a fruit tree simply because it did not have
fruit for him. Some see this as a tale of miraculous power
wasted in the service of an ill-tempered Jesus.

As a result, many commentaries deny this incident and
claim that it is a fictitious miracle story which arose out of
the parable of the unfruitful fig tree in Luke 13:6–9. Mark
11:12–14 becomes more difficult still with the explanatory
comment, "for it was not the season for figs" (Mark 11:13).
Such clauses are a favorite way for Mark to explain certain
things to his readers.[1] Why would Jesus curse a fig tree if
the fig tree could not bear figs at this time of year? Mark's
explanatory comment, at first glance, not only does not
help to understand Jesus' behavior; on the contrary, it
makes it more difficult to understand.

The first thing that can be said in regard to Jesus'
behavior is that to condemn the cursing of a single fig tree
seems like a drastic measure for a society that consumes
millions of trees for the production of pornographic
materials. Can any person eating meat or fish, which
demands the destruction of much higher forms of life,
condemn the destruction of a single fig tree? Neverthe-
less, if Jesus in anger or rage cursed the fig tree for no good

reason, then this action seems to stand in conflict with the general portrayal of Jesus in the New Testament. How can Jesus' behavior be explained?

No answer can be satisfactory if it does not take into consideration Mark's explanatory comment in verse 13 and the arrangement of the materials in Mark 11, 12, and 13. Mark's arrangement of this incident is different than Matthew's. Mark splits this story and places the cleansing of the temple between the two parts. This is a frequent stylistic feature of Mark, evidenced by Mark 3:19–21 and 31–35; 5:21–24 and 35–43; 6:6–13 and 30f.; 14:1–2 and 10–11.

In this instance Mark causes the cursing of the fig tree to "rub off" on the account of the cleansing of the temple. Jesus' cleansing of the temple is understood by Mark not as a reformation of the temple worship but as an act of judgment. The cursing of the fig tree is not an act of Jesus performed in rage against an innocent tree but a symbolic act. It is an acted-out parable, meant to teach his disciples the true meaning of the cleansing of the temple. Both are acts of judgment! The Messiah comes to his temple and instead of the fruit of righteousness he finds nothing but the dry leaves of sterile formalism and hypocrisy, and he judges it. The cursing of the fig tree serves as a symbolic act by which the disciples are to interpret what Jesus is about to do in the temple.

Support for this interpretation comes from observing the arrangement of materials in Mark 11:1–13:32. After the account of the cleansing of the temple (Mark 11:15–19), Mark 11:27–33 contains an account in which Jesus' authority to do this is questioned. The other two Gospels which contain accounts of the cleansing, Matthew and John, are followed by a similar account in which Jesus' authority to do this is questioned. Next, the parable of the wicked tenants (Mark 12:1–11) treats God's judgment on Israel. Mark places this account at this point to reinforce the point he seeks to make in Mark 11:12f. God is about to judge Israel. Immediately following this parable is a fourfold account of Jesus' controversies with his opponents, followed by the story of the widow's mites. Chapter thirteen contains the prophecies of Jesus concerning the destruction of Jerusalem (Mark 13:1–4). In chapters twelve and thirteen Mark gathers various materials to support his interpretation of the cursing of the fig tree and the cleansing of the temple. God is about to bring judgment on Israel.

Interpreting the cursing of the fig tree as an acted parable of the coming judgment also explains the difficult explanatory comment in Mark 11:13. Mark tells us that the cursing of the fig tree is not due to it being fruitless. It was not the time for figs! It must be due to another reason which he points out to his readers. Jesus acts out a parable of judgment for his disciples. The cursing reveals that the cleansing of the temple was an act of judgment! Judgment is coming on Israel. This judgment is further foretold and described in Mark 12:1–11 and 13:1–37.

The cursing of the fig tree ceases to be a problem with this interpretation. It is not an angry act of destruction but a parabolic act of Jesus. There is little difference between Jesus' use of the wood of this tree to symbolize a spiritual truth and in the use of wood to build a manger scene or the use of a cross to decorate the church. The cursing of the fig tree was not a senseless act of rage on the part of Jesus, but the use of a single tree to reveal the truth that judgment was coming. A tree used to teach the truth of God, whether that truth involves the portrayal of the grace of God or the coming judgment, need not be a stumbling block for the believer.

Jesus and the Syrophoenician Woman (Mark 7:24–30)

And from there he arose and went away to the region of Tyre and Sidon. And he entered a house, and would not have any one know it; yet he could not be hid. But immediately a woman, whose little daughter was possessed by an unclean spirit, heard of him, and came and fell down at his feet. Now the woman was a Greek, a Syrophoenician by birth. And she begged him to cast the demon out of her daughter. And he said to her, "Let the children first be fed, for it is not right to take the children's bread and throw it to the dogs." But she answered him, "Yes, Lord; yet even the dogs under the table eat the children's crumbs." And he said to her, "For this saying you may go your way; the demon has left your daughter." And she went home, and found the child lying in bed, and the demon gone.

Mark 7:24–30 and Matthew 15:21–28 contain accounts in which Jesus speaks to a Syrophoenician, or Canaanite, woman. The woman comes to Jesus and begs him to heal her daughter. To this request Jesus replies, "Let the children first be fed, for it is not right to take the children's bread and throw it to the dogs" (Mark 7:27).

The problem is obvious. Jesus' words appear harsh, austere, and insensitive. They seem atypical of Jesus. In the Gospels he is portrayed as kind, loving, and compassionate.[2] The words of Mark 7:27 would cause little difficulty coming from a mean, harsh, and unloving individual. The Jesus of the Gospels, however, is a loving and kind Jesus with special compassion for the outcasts of society and this Gentile woman is an outcast in the Jewish mind![3] The problem in the text is this apparent inconsistency of Jesus' words and behavior with his known character and teachings found throughout the Gospels. This inconsistency should alert us to the possibility that a superficial reading of this text may be incorrect.

A closer examination provides several reasons for not interpreting this text as harsh and unloving. First, neither Mark nor Matthew interpreted it that way. If they were convinced that this passage conflicted with the love of God manifested in Jesus Christ which they had written about in their Gospels, they would not have included this account. If they interpreted this passage as conflicting with the general picture of Jesus they describe in their works, they would have excluded it from their Gospels. After all, not everything which Jesus said and did is recorded in our Gospels (John 20:30–31; 21:25).

Second, the woman in this story is not deterred. She does not think that Jesus' reply is so negative that no response is possible. She senses that a response is possible, perhaps even expected, and she continues with the conversation. It is as if she sees in Jesus' reply a kind of riddle which challenges her to respond.

Third, Jesus' reply presents two terms which soften the apparent harshness of his words. The first is not apparent in the English translation. It involves the term *dogs*. In Greek the term is *kunaria*. If Jesus wanted to refer to wild stray dogs, scavengers, he would have used a different term, *kunes*. His use of the former term means that he is talking about pet household dogs or puppies, not curs. (The use of *kunaria* rather than *kunes* also reveals that the idea that for Jews all Gentiles were "dogs" should not be brought into this analogy. Gentiles were "dogs" in the sense of *kunes* not *kunaria!*) If the expression "dogs" is replaced with the expression "puppies," a great deal of the apparent harshness is removed.

The second term found in Mark's text is *first*. This implies that "puppies" can be fed after all. Jesus did not say, "Let the children *only* be fed. . . ." He said, "Let the children *first* be fed. . . ." This term also removes a great deal of the apparent harshness. Undoubtedly these terms provided encouragement for the Syrophoenician woman, and she continued to engage Jesus in conversation.

Finally, it should be noted that Jesus spoke with the woman prior to this point. The text states, "And he said to her" (Mark 7:27). The Greek verb used is *elegen*. This is the imperfect tense in Greek and indicates there is a running conversation between Jesus and the woman ("and Jesus was saying to her").[4]

The parallel account, Matt. 15:22–25, also indicates that this is part of a continuing dialogue between Jesus and the Syrophoenician woman. Jesus' words are not a one-line rejection of the woman's request. Mark 7:27 contains words spoken in the middle of a dialogue. The woman's response indicates that she, in light of this conversation, assumes that the dialogue is not over. The text seems to suggest that the woman senses that she is expected to respond to these words.

One of the unfortunate liabilities of written speech is the fact that the tone of voice cannot be recorded. In conversation a change in tone, a wink, a pause, or a smile suggest how the words are to be interpreted. This text uttered with a frown would mean something quite different than if it were uttered with a wink or a smile. The former would mean, "Be off! Don't bother me, for it is not right to take the children's bread and throw it to the dogs!" In the latter instance it would mean, "It is not right to take the children's bread and throw it to the dogs, is it? What do you think?"

In the absence of voice tone, these words of Jesus must be interpreted with any verbal hints the verse contains and in the context of Jesus' life and teachings. In light of the verbal hints mentioned above (the terms *puppies, first,* and *elegen*—"he was saying"), the response of the woman, and the character of Jesus found in this Gospel and all the Gospels, it seems best to interpret the text as a match of wits in which Jesus seeks to lead the Syrophoenician woman to a more persistent and deeper faith. This he accomplishes. Her reply, "Yes, Lord; yet even the dogs under the table eat the children's crumbs" (Mark 7:28) brings the following response, "For this saying you may go your way; the demon has left your daughter" (Mark 7:29).[5]

Jesus and Mary Magdalene After the Resurrection
(John 20:17)

A final example of difficult actions of Jesus takes place on Easter morning. After Mary Magdalene recognizes Jesus, he says to her in John 20:17, "Do not hold me, for I have not yet ascended to the Father; but go to my brethren and say to them, I am ascending to my Father and your Father, to my God and your God." The difficulty lies in the fact that later Jesus bids Thomas, "Put your finger here, and see my hands; and put out your hand, and place it in my side; do not be faithless, but believing" (John 20:27).[6]

Why is Mary forbidden to "touch" Jesus (KJV) whereas Thomas, one week later, is not only permitted to touch Jesus but is invited to touch his wounds? The difficulty with this verse is compounded by the fact that Mary is not to touch or hold Jesus because he has not yet ascended to the Father. Thomas is invited to do so even though Jesus still has not ascended.

Numerous suggestions have been made on how to interpret this verse:

1. Mary is not to touch Jesus because his wounds have not yet healed.
2. Mary is not to touch Jesus in order that she not be ceremonially defiled by touching a "dead" body.
3. Mary holds on to Jesus in order to have him give her holy communion. She did not participate in the Last Supper along with the disciples.
4. Mary is not to touch Jesus because he left his grave clothes behind and is naked.
5. Mary is not showing sufficient respect to Jesus' glorified body.
6. The Greek text of John 20:17 has been amended or changed. Instead of reading "touch not" (*me haptou*), it is made to read "fear not" (*me ptoou*). According to this view an error was made by the Evangelist, or

someone before him, and Jesus' actual words were
mistranslated in John 20:17.
7. Mary is not to hold on to Jesus because Jesus is not
   ascending to the Father immediately.

It often is easier to see incorrect interpretations of the
passage than to discover the correct one!

First, it should be observed that the translation "Touch
me not," (KJV) is not found in newer translations. The
Revised Standard Version states, "Do not hold me"; the
New International Version, "Do not hold on to me"; the
New English Bible, the Jerusalem Bible, and the New King
James Version, "Do not cling to me"; and the New
American Standard Bible, "Stop clinging to me." The
newer translations are clearly correct. The negative par-
ticle in the Greek text (*me*) used with a present imperative
indicates a prohibition to stop doing something Mary is
already doing. Mary is told by Jesus to "Stop clinging/
holding me," not "Do not begin to touch me."

This command can be understood in one of two ways.
First, the prohibition is tied closely with the command to
go and tell the disciples. "Time is wasting away. Stop
holding me, but go tell the disciples. . . ." This interpretation does not deal with the phrase, "for I have not yet
ascended to the Father." This latter phrase is difficult.
Does it imply that holding on to Jesus after his ascension
would be acceptable? It would appear that after the
ascension, holding the exalted Lord would be even more
inappropriate.

Perhaps the best interpretation is: Mary has been clinging on to Jesus due to the joy that Jesus is indeed alive,
that he has "revived." She sought to resume the former
relationship that she had with the rabbi, Jesus of Nazareth. (Note Mary's address to Jesus in John 20:16 of
"Rab-boni," or teacher.) But, Jesus has not simply been
resuscitated; he has been raised from the dead and is now
Lord![7] C. K. Barrett states, "Both by her address to Jesus as

teacher, and physical contact, she is trying to recapture the past."[8]

The prohibition of Jesus is due to the mistaken understanding of Mary. With Thomas this was not a problem. John 20:28 reveals that he recognizes Jesus not as Rab-boni but as "My Lord and my God." The clause, "for I have not yet ascended to the Father," serves to reveal to Mary that the old relationship must give way to a new one. Jesus is now the risen Lord and must ascend into the presence of the Father. This passage can be paraphrased: "Mary, stop clinging to me. The situation has changed. I have been raised from the dead as Lord, and I am about to go to be with the Father. But go and tell the disciples. . . ."

Notes

1. Note Mark 1:16, 22; 2:15; 3:10, 21; 6:14; 7:3; etc.
2. Cf. Mark 6:34, 8:2; Matthew 9:36; Luke 7:13; etc.
3. Cf. Luke 15:1f.; Mark 2:16.
4. Compare the other three instances of this same verbal form in this chapter. In Mark 7:9, 14, 20 they are all dealing with a continuing conversation between the parties involved.
5. Compare Matthew 15:28 where the response of Jesus is, " 'O woman, great is your faith! Be it done for you as you desire.' "
6. Cf. Luke 24:39; Matthew 28:9.
7. Note Acts 2:32–33; Romans 1:4; Philippians 2:9–11.
8. C. K. Barrett, *The Gospel According to St. John* (Philadelphia: Westminster, 1978), p. 565.

4

Difficulties in the Predictions of Jesus

The final chapter deals with three sayings of Jesus. These sayings were not discussed in chapter two, which deals with difficult sayings of Jesus, because they form a specific and unique category. These three sayings are predictions of Jesus which do not appear to have come to pass! All three predictions appear to refer to events that were to be fulfilled in Jesus' lifetime or at his resurrection. At first glance, at least, they were not.

Jesus' Being Three Days and Three Nights in the Heart of the Earth (Matt. 12:38–40)

> Then some of the scribes and Pharisees said to him, "Teacher, we wish to see a sign from you." But he answered them, "An evil and adulterous generation seeks for a sign; but no sign shall be given to it except the sign of the prophet Jonah. For as Jonah was three days and three nights in the belly of the whale, so will the Son of man be three days and three nights in the heart of the earth."

It is clear that Jesus rejects the call to perform various signs before the Jewish religious leadership in order to justify his claims and actions.[1] Jesus would not give them signs, however, for he did not come to be a wonder-worker but a Savior. Jesus performed many miracles in private and with a warning not to tell others about them.[2] Yet, one great miracle would be given as a sign. This would be the "sign of Jonah," his resurrection from the "heart of the earth."

The main problem encountered in Matthew 12:38–40 involves the temporal designation "three days and three nights." Interpreting this designation literally, some argue that Jesus was crucified on Thursday rather than Friday. A Friday crucifixion and a Sunday resurrection do not provide sufficient time for three days and three nights.

There are numerous ways of figuring out the day-night scheme for this period of time, but it is clear that three separate days and nights cannot be obtained by a Friday crucifixion and Sunday resurrection scheme. Yet, it is clear from the Gospels that Jesus was crucified on Friday, the ". . . day of Preparation, that is, the day before the sabbath" (Mark 15:42) and raised on Sunday, the ". . . first day of the week . . ." (Mark 16:2). If the temporal designation of Matthew 12:40 is taken literally, a conflict does exist between the time indicated in this verse and the time indicated in the accounts of the passion story.

But should the expression "three days and three nights" be interpreted literally? Three arguments indicate that it should not. First, it appears that this expression is another way of stating "on the third day" or "in three days." This can be illustrated from 1 Samuel 30:12–13. The same Greek expression is found in 1 Samuel 30:12 in the Greek translation of the Old Testament (the LXX) as in Matthew 12:40. Verse 13 refers to this three-day and three-night period as "three days ago" or, as the LXX literally states, "the third day today." If "three days and three nights" can mean "on the third day," there is no major problem in our passage. By Jewish reckoning Jesus could have been crucified on Friday and raised on Sunday, the third day. Friday afternoon = day one; Friday 6

P.M. to Saturday 6 P.M. = day two; Saturday 6 P.M. to Sunday 6 P.M. = day three.[3]

A second argument against a literal temporal interpretation is the fact that Matthew did not see any conflict between this expression and either a third-day resurrection (Matt. 16:21; 17:23; 20:19) or a Friday crucifixion and Sunday resurrection scheme (Matt. 27:62; 28:1). For him, as well as for the other Evangelists, expressions such as "three days and three nights," "after three days," and "on the third day" could be used interchangeably.

Finally, it should be pointed out that the main point of Jesus' analogy in Matthew 12:40 does not involve the temporal designation but the sign of the resurrection. Only one miracle or sign will be given to this evil and adulterous generation. That sign will be Jesus' resurrection from the dead. The temporal designation is much less significant. Perhaps Jesus refers to three days and three nights because this expression is found in the Old Testament passage which he wants to quote (Jonah 1:17).

Understood in the context of biblical Judaism, the designation "three days and three nights" poses no problem with the Friday crucifixion and Sunday resurrection scheme described in the passion narratives. It is only if a twentieth-century reckoning of time is imposed or if the idiomatic nature of this temporal designation is not understood that a problem appears.

Seeing the Angels Ascending and Descending Upon the Son of Man (John 1:51)

Another passage with a prediction of Jesus which does not appear to have taken place is John 1:51. "And he [Jesus] said to him, 'Truly, truly, I say to you, you will see heaven opened, and the angels of God ascending and descending upon the Son of man.'"

The problem in this verse is self-evident. Where, in the life of Jesus, is it recorded that angels literally ascend and descend on him? Attempts to resolve this difficulty fall into one of two classifications: (1) attempts to interpret this passage literally; and (2) attempts to interpret this passage metaphorically.

Several attempts have been made to establish a literal interpretation of this verse. Some commentators see a reference to the angels who ministered to Jesus during his Temptation. However, there is no account of the Temptation in John. If this passage refers to the Temptation, it would be expected the Evangelist would refer to such an account. Furthermore, this verse refers to a future event ("you will see"). At this point in Jesus' ministry the incident of the Temptation, which is only recorded in the Synoptic Gospels, would be a past event.

Another "literal" interpretation has been to see a reference to the resurrection of Jesus. All four Gospels refer to angels present at the empty tomb. Yet their presence does not appear to fulfil the reference to the "angels of God ascending and descending upon the Son of man." John gives no hint that this verse refers to the resurrection.

A final literal interpretation is to see a reference to the *parousia*, or second coming. Jesus' return is frequently associated with accompanying angels.[4] The wording of the text concerning angels "ascending and descending upon the Son of man" seems strange if the *parousia* is meant and John does not specifically refer to angels being present at the *parousia*.

In the absence of any event in John, or in the Synoptic Gospels, which resembles the fulfillment of a literal interpretation of this verse, it is not surprising that many interpreters seek a non-literal or metaphorical meaning. It is evident that John (and Jesus) were inclined to use metaphorical language. The many "I am" sayings found in his Gospel point this out.[5] It would not be surprising to see that John interprets this passage in a metaphorical way. This possibility is enhanced by the fact that this text is a clear reference to Genesis 28:12, "And he [Jacob] dreamed that there was a ladder set up on the earth, and the top of it reached to heaven; and behold, the angels of God were ascending and descending on it!" Apparently Augustine first made reference to this Genesis passage in which the same order of "ascending and descending" is found.

In the Genesis account this vision of Jacob is connected to a revelatory event. The God of Abraham and Isaac appears to Jacob and reveals that he will renew with him the covenant he made with Abraham and Isaac. This incident and vision of the angels ascending and descending upon Jacob is associated with revelatory matters. The Midrash Rabbah (an ancient Jewish commentary on Genesis) associates this passage with Sinai and with Moses and Aaron ("the angels of God") ascending ("Moses went up to God") and descending ("Moses went down from the mount").[6] It is not surprising that John 1:51 is frequently interpreted as a reference to the revelation of God in or to Christ.

There are other metaphorical interpretations of this verse. Some suggest that this verse refers to Jesus' baptism where heaven opens to Jesus and Jesus has direct access to the revelation of God. There are two strong objections to this interpretation. First, the Gospel of John contains no specific reference to Jesus' baptism. Again, such a reference would be expected if John interpreted the text in this manner. Second, the baptism of Jesus is a past event when these words are spoken and Jesus uses a future tense ("will see").

Another suggestion is that Jesus is the "gate of heaven,"[7] the place of God's grace upon earth, or the tent of God among men (John 1:14). Similarly, others interpret this text to mean that Jesus is the link between heaven and earth.[8] In a more general way this verse is interpreted as teaching that the Son of man is the "place" of the full revelation of God. It is in Jesus Christ that God fully manifests his glory and revelation. This latter interpretation seems attractive. It is clear that for John the glory of God is manifested in Jesus (John 2:11; 11:40). To behold Jesus in faith is to have an open door to heaven and to the revelation of God (John 14:8–31), even as Jacob in Genesis 28:12 had an open door to heaven and the revelation of God. It is not primarily in Jacob and the covenant God made with him that the greater revelation of God is now found. It is in Jesus, the Son of man, that such revelation is found.

This interpretation fits well the next account found in the Gospel of John. In John 2:1–11 Jesus performs his first miracle. John states, "This, the first of his signs, Jesus did at Cana in Galilee, and manifested his glory; and his disciples believed in him" (John 2:11). Metaphorically understood, the angels of God ascend and descend upon the Son of man as he manifests here (and on other occasions) his glory as the only begotten Son of God.

The Son of Man Coming During the Lifetime of the Disciples (Matt. 10:23)

The final passage causes numerous problems in its interpretation. In Matthew 10:23b Jesus states, "for truly, I say to you, you will not have gone through all the towns of Israel, before the Son of man comes." On this passage Albert Schweitzer based his view that Jesus expected the kingdom of God to come during his ministry. When it did not come he was greatly disappointed. As a result he sought to force God's hand and make him bring the kingdom only to be even more bitterly disappointed and cry out in despair on the cross, "My God, my God, why hast thou forsaken me!" (Matt. 27:46).

The problem that this text raises is clear. If Jesus is referring to his second coming and if this is said to his disciples as they are going out on a preaching mission (Matt. 10:1 and 5 give that impression), then the evangelical Christian encounters a real problem. The second coming obviously did not take place during the mission of the disciples!

Numerous attempts have been made to resolve this problem. It has been suggested that the "coming of the Son of man" could refer to: the spread of the gospel throughout the world; the gradual recognition of Jesus as King and the establishment of his reign on the earth; the fall of Jerusalem as a sign of Jesus' judgment upon unbelieving Israel; or the coming of the Spirit on the disciples during this mission. Calvin favored the latter explanation.[9]

All these attempts to alleviate this problem seek to do so at the expense of the clear meaning of the text. In light of the other references to the coming of the Son of man in Matthew, it is clear that this passage refers to the second coming of Christ.[10]

It is especially important to judge carefully the context in which this verse is found. Although Matthew 10:5–42 looks like a simple mission charge of Jesus to his disciples it is clearly more than this. Why would Matthew devote so much space to a mission charge to the disciples unless it had relevance for the church of his own day as well? Matthew understood that Jesus' instructions to the disciples were a pattern for his own day, and he took those instructions and added other teachings of Jesus spoken on other occasions. As a result Matthew 10:5 ("Go nowhere among the Gentiles, and enter no town of the Samaritans, but go rather to the lost sheep of the house of Israel.") is clearly a specific reference to this mission of the disciples during Jesus' ministry. After the resurrection the Christian mission is to all the world (Matt. 28:18–20).

Other relevant teachings that Jesus spoke elsewhere were included by Matthew in this mission charge. These include a section on persecution for the sake of Christ (10:16–25) and the conditions of discipleship (10:26–42). It is evident that the section in which the passage under consideration is found looks beyond the immediate situation of the disciples because: (1) the reference to appearing before governors and kings, for the disciples' mission was only to the lost sheep of Israel and not the regions of the Gentiles or Samaritans (10:5–6); and (2) the language of 10:17–18;[11] 10:19;[12] and 10:21–22[13] which portray not merely times of persecution but the time of the Great Persecution. Matthew therefore uses the mission of the disciples in Jesus' day as an opportunity to teach about future missions and persecutions that Christians will encounter for the cause of Christ.

This understanding of the arrangement of this chapter by Matthew is supported by the overall arrangement found in the Gospel of Matthew. Matthew arranged his Gospel carefully and quite artistically. He arranged the teachings (T) of Jesus into five blocks and surrounded them with six narrative (N) sections: N (1–4); T (5–7); N (8–9); T (10); N (11–12); T (13); N (14–17); T (18); N (19–23); T (24–25); N(26–28). From this arrangement it seems reasonable to conclude that the teachings found in these five blocks (one of which is Matthew 10) are collections of Jesus' teachings which Matthew arranged according to theme rather than chronology.

It appears reasonable to assume that Matthew 10:23b need not have been said to the disciples as they went out on their mission. It is a saying of Jesus that could have been said on a different occasion and brought into the present context of chapter ten by Matthew. In the immediate context of this verse, the theme involves persecution for the sake of Jesus. Interspersed with the warnings of such persecution are three words of encouragement and hope. The first involves the fact that the followers of Jesus need not be concerned at such times with the response they should give to their persecutors because the Holy Spirit will give them the words to say (10:19–20). (It should be noted that this is advice given to prospective martyrs and not to pastors for Sunday morning worship services!) The second word is the passage disciples in Jesus' under consideration (10:23b). The third word is the realization that in so suffering they will be following in the footsteps of Jesus (10:24–25).

Therefore, Matthew 10:23b should be interpreted not as a prediction that the Son of man will return before the disciples finish their mission to Israel, but as a word of encouragement in the context of future persecutions or especially in the context of the Future Persecution. It is clear that this is the way that Matthew understood this. He wrote his Gospel after the mission of the disciples and after Jesus' lifetime, and the Son of man had not yet come. It is unlikely that he interpreted this passage as a reference to the second coming during the ministry of Jesus.

Furthermore, how could the coming of the Son of man from heaven take place during the ministry of Jesus? Matthew believed that Jesus was the Son of man and the saying in the text refers to the coming of the Son of man while Jesus was still alive. Matthew clearly did not believe that Jesus told the disciples that before they finished their mission, the second coming would take place. Jesus had not yet ascended into heaven when he spoke these words.

It is true that certain critical scholars suggest that Jesus did not teach that he was the Son of man but that the Son of man was someone else. Therefore Jesus refers to that other Son of man's coming during his ministry. Such a reconstruction is a rejection of the present context of Matthew in favor of a hypothetically reconstructed one that can never be proven. It must assume that Jesus speaks of someone else as being the Son of man. The latter assumption is confronted with the fact that nowhere in the New Testament is there any indication that any writer understands that the Son of man is anyone other than Jesus.

It appears that Jesus' words (". . . for truly, I say to you, you will not have gone through all the towns of Israel, before the Son of man comes") are not a reference to the coming of the Son of man during the mission of the lifetime. The context suggests that another interpretation is preferable. This text can be interpreted as a word of promise and reassurance that during the Tribulation, as the believer flees from place to place, he will not run out of places to flee to. Before this takes place the Son of man will return![14]

Notes

1. Cf. Matthew 16:1–4; Mark 8:11–12; Luke 23:8–9; etc.

2. Cf. Mark 1:40–45, 5:35–43, 7:31–36, etc.

3. Cf. Luke 24:31 where the two disciples on the road to Emmaus say on Easter Sunday, "It is now the third day since this (the crucifixion) happened."

4. Cf. Mark 8:38, 13:26–27; Matthew 25:31; etc.

5. Cf. John 6:35, 51; 8:12; 10:7, 11; 11:25; etc.

6. The *Midrash Rabbah* on Genesis 28:12.

7. Cf. Genesis 28:17 and John 10:7–9; 14:6.

8. Cf. John 3:13.

9. John Calvin, *A Harmony of the Evangelists Matthew, Mark, and Luke,* ed., David W. and Thomas F. Torrance (Grand Rapids: Eerdmans, 1972), on Matthew 10:23.

10. See Matthew 16:27–28; 24:27, 30, 37, 39, 44; 25:31; 26:64.

11. Cf. Mark 13:9/Luke 21:12.

12. Cf. Mark 13:11/Luke 21:14–15.

13. Cf. Mark 13:12–13/Luke 21:16–17.

14. Cf. Matthew 24:21–22; 1 Corinthians 10:13.

Conclusion

In these four chapters various kinds of problems found in the Gospels are discussed. Certainly not all the problems or difficulties found in these four works are treated; and undoubtedly many readers would desire that a specific passage that troubles them would be discussed. This book attempts to treat a representative number of passages in the hope that they will typify the kind of problems encountered in reading the Gospels.

Many problems that arise in reading the Gospels are due to some basic misconception on the part of the modern-day reader. One major difficulty is that the reader often misunderstands the form of Jesus' teachings. He tries to interpret literally what to Jesus was a nonliteral literary form. An example of this is not recognizing the use of hyperbole or overstatement on the part of Jesus. The problems some readers have with regard to various teachings of Jesus such as his teaching on swearing (p. 63) or prayer (p. 77) is primarily due to interpreting literally what Jesus intends as an exaggeration for effect. Not recognizing Jesus' use of metaphor, as in the "sword" saying (p. 84), or the idiomatic nature of some of his teachings, as in the case of his reference to "three days and three nights" (p. 113), the "angels ascending and descending" (p. 115), or the phrase "lead us not into temptation" (p. 70) can also cause problems. Again, the

123

difficulty does not lie in the saying but in the ability to understand what Jesus meant by the saying. The use of a symbolic action, as in the case of his cursing of the fig tree (p. 103), and the use of parables also creates problems for the reader. A tendency to allegorize the parables and press the details for meaning causes great confusion when parables such as the parable of the unjust steward (p. 80) or the rich man and Lazarus (p. 88) are interpreted. These troubles disappear when the parables are treated as teaching by way of analogy one main point.

Perhaps the greatest problem that the reader today faces when reading the Gospels is that he usually brings a preconceived notion of what the Evangelists should or must have done in writing these inspired works. Sometimes by reasoning backwards from a doctrine of Biblical inspiration it is easy to predetermine how the Evangelists must have written their works. For some Christians the doctrines of biblical infallibility and inerrancy require that all the material in the Gospels must be arranged in strictly chronological order with twentieth-century scientific goals. Yet is it possible to impose on the inspired Evangelists a modern sense of how they should have written? If it is believed that the Evangelists were inspired by God and are thus infallible and inerrant in all they wrote, should it not be possible to learn from them and by the way they wrote?

Great defenders of the faith, such as Augustine and John Calvin, understood that at times the material in the Gospels is arranged topically. The Evangelists often arranged their material according to subject matter rather than according to chronology. This is especially true of various teachings of Jesus which originally circulated as independent units. For them the truth of Jesus' beatitudes, metaphors, or parables, is not dependent on knowing exactly when they were uttered. As a result they were able to accept the topical arrangement of many of Jesus' teachings. If the believer accepts this truth, many of the difficulties encountered in the Gospels can be resolved. This is even more important if it is realized that the Evangelists arranged certain similar stories of Jesus, such as his miracles, in topical rather than chronological order. If this is accepted Christians need not postulate that Jesus raised Jairus's daughter from the dead on two separate occasions. We can simply acknowledge that the Evangelists placed this miracle of Jesus at different places in their Gospels.

Of all the kinds of problems encountered in the Gospels, the most evident and the most difficult are those in which parallel passages in various Gospels appear slightly different. It is not surprising that these difficulties have been dealt with the most in the history of the church and in this book. In fact the term *harmonize* is primarily used with this kind of problem where the difficulties in parallel passages are "harmonized."

If the Christian can accept that the Evangelists were permitted to be inspired interpreters of Jesus' teachings, and were not simply stenographers, numerous difficulties disappear. Thus the minor variations in wording—such as in the first beatitude (p. 20), or the change in audience of the parable of the lost sheep (p. 46)—no longer pose problems but are assets in seeking to understand the significance for today of such teachings of Jesus. Also, if the believer is aware that the Evangelists did not come out of a similar scientific training but sought to convey the infallible truth of God in a way that their readers could understand, then additional problems also disappear. As a result the mention or lack of mention of various messengers in the healing of the centurion's servant (p. 26), the telescoping of conversation in the raising of Jairus's daughter (p. 30), or the apparent difference in roof construction materials in the healing of the paralytic (p. 34) no longer pose major problems. It is satisfying to learn that great defenders of the evangelical faith such as Augustine and John Calvin came to similar conclusions.

No attempt has been made in this work to claim that the various explanations and interpretations given are infallible. God is infallible; scholars are not! A teacher or writer is infallible only to the degree that his teaching is in accord with the infallible teachings of God's Word. It is hoped that some of the solutions to difficult passages in the Gospels will help the reader. Even more than this, it is hoped that the method for treating such difficulties will be useful to the reader.

If some of the solutions suggested in this work do not seem to be honoring or truthful to the inspired Scriptures, then it is prayed that the reader will seek—like Augustine, Calvin, and other defenders of the faith—to devise a better solution that will be true to the Word of God.

However, remember two things. First, be true to the meaning of the text. Seek to understand the conscious meaning of the biblical author as it is expressed in the words of the text. Second, be open to the possibility that it may not be possible to understand or to explain a text. Such a confession is not necessarily the result of a weak doctrine of inspiration. It is a confession of human creatureliness.

The Scriptures are infallible because the writers were inspired by an infallible God as they wrote them. But understanding and attempted resolutions may not be inerrant because they come from fallible and fallen creatures. Humility at times forces Christians to confess that they do not have a completely satisfactory solution. Such a confession also believes that if sufficient information were available, this apparent difficulty could also be explained.